# The New Financial Advisor

## *Strategies for Successful Family Wealth Management*

**G. SCOTT BUDGE, PhD**

**WILEY**
John Wiley & Sons, Inc.

Published by John Wiley & Sons, Inc., Hoboken, New Jersey.
Published simultaneously in Canada.

For general information on our other products and services or for technical support,
please contact our Customer Care Department within the United States at
(800) 762-2974, outside the United States at (317) 572-3993 or fax (317) 572-4002.

Wiley also publishes its books in a variety of electronic formats. Some content that
appears in print may not be available in electronic books. For more information about
Wiley products, visit our web site at www.wiley.com.

**_Library of Congress Cataloging-in-Publication Data_**

Budge, G. Scott, 1956–
    The new financial advisor : strategies for successful family wealth management /
G. Scott Budge.
        p.   cm.
    Includes bibliographical references and index.
    ISBN 978-0-470-27530-6 (cloth)
    1. Financial planners.   2. Investment advisors.   3. Financial planning industry.
I. Title.
    HG179.5.B83 2008
    332.024—dc22

                                                                2008012001

Printed in the United States of America.

10   9   8   7   6   5   4   3   2   1

To the memory of my dear daughter, Zoë Claire Lamb-Budge

# Contents

# Preface

The tide has changed. The roles and responsibilities of financial advisors opposite their private clients have expanded in depth and importance in ways that could only be dimly seen even a decade ago. From product purveyors to solution providers to agents of change, financial advisors find themselves facing a new competitive demand that they become ever more sophisticated in the psychology and dynamics of families. This book is aimed squarely at that challenge, namely, that the new financial advisor is, like it or not, in the business of changing lives.

This has been true to a degree all along, but it is only recently that the ability to thoughtfully deliver advice and services in ways that make a meaningful impact on the lives of clients has become a critical source of competitive differentiation. Financial service marketing and advertising has helped generate the expectation that financial advisors will be among the most trusted advisors in clients' worlds, and that their job is to facilitate the attainment of life goals. Knowing the difficulty of differentiating on performance and product, they have shifted the messages clients hear from product-centric messaging to everything from how to raise financially fit kids and run family meetings to how to manage finances through divorce, retirement, and other major life transitions. Expectations have also arisen as both advisors and their clients share in the notion that financial products have, for the most part, become completely commoditized.

What hasn't happened are those changes the advisor on the street needs to make in order to step confidently into this new role, a role that is part therapist and part priest, as well as one requiring the conventional skills of financial and wealth management. This is the new financial advisor: a wealth manager where wealth is now defined as the sum total of resources—human as well as financial—that can be brought to bear on a life objective.

Thus, this work is about taking the dialogue about advisor effectiveness to a new level, and about closing the gap between what is increasingly being promised by the new imagery of the financial advisor and what it actually means to practice day in and day out as a new financial advisor.

Jay Hughes has elegantly framed the role choices in his depiction of the difference between what he calls the *personne d'affaires* and the *personne de confiance* in the wealth management space. The *personne d'affaires* is a purveyor of financial goods and services, and may be a relatively well-trusted part of the family-advisory system. The *personne de confiance*, however, takes the next step by evolving from this role into that of an advisor who is the deepest confidant to whom the family begins to turn for all major forms of leadership and assistance. Only a few will become *personnes de confiances*. They will completely unhook from product-based revenue and will work for only one or a few families as they look at dynastic family matters in 100-year time frames. This work supports this concept while also embracing the idea that even those who will never assume the role of *personnes de confiances* will have a need to increase their sophistication with respect to family dynamics and the various ways in which family life and financial life are inextricably intertwined.

To accomplish the admittedly ambitious task of raising the bar with respect to the skills of the family wealth manager, we follow a basic logic that centers on those things that will support the day-to-day movement of the new financial advisor in the direction of greater enlightenment about and efficacy with families. This means discussing the psychology of money and wealth, as well as the personal knowledge of the advisor of his or her own dynamics in relation to the "loaded" issues clients bring. But it also means examining life transitions clients go through, and changes to the service model and economics in this new space. The implications of this for financial institutions and for thinking about ethics are addressed, particularly as the impact of the advisor's new role affects a widening range of stakeholders, sometimes profoundly and in unanticipated ways.

The new financial advisor has much to consider beyond the core disciplines from which they come. Deep knowledge of investments, financial planning, estate planning, and risk management is necessary but insufficient for more and more advisors facing into the emerging frontiers of family wealth management. It is an exciting frontier, laced with risks but pregnant with opportunities for those rising to the challenge of getting more sophisticated in developing and nesting solutions in dynamic client systems.

# Acknowledgments

This book rests on the shoulders of many individuals. In many ways, I have to track my tenure with SEI Investments as profoundly influential on my thinking about the matters of this book. In particular, 10 years ago Al West created the conditions in which some of the proto-ideas behind my thinking could pick up speed. He in turn directed me to Gil Beebower, who gave me my first reading list in behavioral economics even as they were doing due diligence on a new firm called LSV Asset Management.

I also owe much to the following who I have rubbed shoulders with over many years, including Jane Abitanta, Karen Adler, Libby Anderson, Patricia Angus, Charlotte Beyer, Philip Boxer, Olivia Boyce-Abel, Charlie Collier, Francois de Visccher, Maryann Fernandez, Scott Fithian, Todd Fithian, Lee Hausner, Fredda Herz-Brown, Tom Holland, Ed Hoover, Jay Hughes, Dennis Jaffe, Dirk Jungé, Stephen Kitching, Patricia LeBon, Kathryn McCarthy, Paul McKibbin, Rosemary McGarrity, Drew Mendoza, Bonnie Mills, Edward Monte, Jim Murphy, Maria Neary, Bob Nigro, Paola Oviedo, Stephen Rolfe, Evan Roth, Mark Rubin, Paul Schervish, Susan Shively, Skip Shuda, Jeffrey Sprowles, Bente Strong, Kay Wakefield, Michael Walkup, Eric Wasserman, Keith Whitaker, Peter White and Bill White.

Thanks must also go to Bob Diforio of D4EO Literary Agency and to the team at Wiley, especially Debra Englander, Kelly O'Connor, and Stacey Small, who helped bring this project to fruition.

The members of the Ackerman Institute's Money and Family Life project have also been very supportive over the years as we've attempted to chart some of this terrain and its implications for us all personally and professionally. Many thanks to Judith Stern Peck, Greg Rogers, Shira Ronen, Sally Wigutow, Elizabeth Bailey, Marcia Sheinberg, Peter Steinglass, Jeffrey Fischer, and Susan Burden.

Finally, this book would have never happened without the palpable support of Henrietta E. Renzi through all the ups and downs of this entire endeavor. Thanks to you, Hen.

# About the Author

G. Scott Budge, Ph.D. is a managing director at RayLign Advisory, LLC, a Greenwich, Connecticut–based advisor to multigenerational families and their advisors. He is an expert in the dynamics of wealthy families, having worked directly with hundreds of entrepreneurs, corporate executives and their families. Prior to joining RayLign, Scott founded two companies focused on delivering Internet-based management services to single- and multifamily offices, and financial advisors throughout the United States and Canada. In addition, he was a Senior Vice President at SEI Investments where he codeveloped their family wealth management unit and participated in several multiyear strategic projects. Scott has published several articles, including works on the psychology of investments, family wealth, and family businesses, and has served on the editorial board of the *Family Business Review*. He has also spoken at numerous industry conferences in the United States, Europe, the Caribbean, and Latin America. In addition, Scott was a founder and member of the creative team at Shaking the Tree Foundation, a professional theater group whose productions focus on challenges faced by families of wealth. Scott is a Fellow at the Family Firm Institute, a founding member of the Money and Family Life Project at the Ackerman Institute for the Family, and holds a PhD in psychology from New York University.

# INTRODUCTION

# Where We Are and How
# It Got That Way

You didn't ask to be in this situation.

You've just left an intense meeting with a client. Your college and graduate school studies, your Series 7, 65, 24, your CFP, CPA, MBA, or CFA—none of this prepared you for what just happened, where your long-standing client and his wife had sharp words with each other about the causes of their daughter's reckless spending behavior. No less, this behavior occurred during a routine, semiannual meeting in which you were prepared to present the couple with strong after-tax results on their combined portfolios. This meeting should have been a breeze, but the air became thick with tension when you asked your clients casually about how the kids were doing now that the eldest was off to college. More awkward still was the peculiar role the couple placed you in as they looked to you for answers, not about whether the portfolio should be rebalanced or whether they were overexposed to alternative asset classes, but about what they should do about their daughter. Oddly cast as part priest, judge, and sage, you closed the meeting uneasily and wondered why this seemed to be happening over and over these days with your financial clients.

Like it or not, your role as a financial advisor is changing. Unlike earlier eras, you now operate deep in the heart of your clients' lives and have become one of the most important beachheads of intervention into the health and well-being of families. Priests, psychologists, accountants, physicians, and lawyers—to name a few—all assume tactical, trusted roles with families. Yet because of your unique pathway to a family's most private issues and conundrums surrounding their finances, you are increasingly part of an advance guard intervening on families. What you do affects families, in many cases profoundly and in unanticipated ways—for better or worse. Beyond sexuality, health, and spirituality lies that profoundly private, tangled, and taboo topic of money, something that financial advisors—from accountants and financial planners to investment advisors and estate attorneys—often

1

feel ill-equipped to deal with using the mundane logic and tools of their disciplines.

Most advisors know this feeling on some level. You also understand the responsibility this entails and have developed competencies to build deeper and more profound relationships with your clients. At the same time, many of you are reluctant travelers at various points along this journey. Some advisors deny that they are anything other than investment advisors or accountants in the same professional silos. Another set realizes they're in deep—like a deer in the headlights—and become struck by the realization that what they learned in school did not prepare them for where they are. Still others look to an emerging set of tools hitting the market that support such things as values-based financial and charitable planning. These tools both support and anesthetize the advisor temporarily, but do not stave off the larger wave of changes shifting their role in their clients' lives.

There are various stances that can be taken opposite these changes, some of them productive and some defensive. They might include:

- *Product guru.* You've developed genuine product expertise, which means your challenge is how to nest your product in someone else who is working on the life-outcomes side of the relationship.
- *Expert.* You approach your client families as an expert, which means your challenge will lie in figuring out how to enable families to develop *their own expertise* over family financial decision making.
- *Macho.* You relegate all of these new client-side demands to "soft side" providers, which means your challenge will forever be defending against becoming irrelevant and a Wall Street caricature.
- *Ostrich.* You systematically, if unconsciously, ignore new messages your clients and the industry are sending you, which means your challenge will be to do something other than cling to existing, self-selecting clients who remain the minority of clients who do not demand more from their advisors.
- *Salesman.* For you, everything is a sale and a deal, which means that your challenge will be to avoid becoming a bit player in the delivery of advice and service—the twin areas providing the most opportunity for competitive differentiation.[1]

Once out of bounds, it is now routine to see institutions such as CitiGroup's Global Private Bank now explicitly include the following in its description of services:

> *Family Advisory Practice provides clients with access to professional advice and expertise on inheritance, succession planning, issues of family unity, raising children in affluence, and supporting foundations, all of which can impact your long-term financial strategies.*

Firms like Merrill Lynch are giving more than investment advice, as in the blurb below abstracted from the home page of its Advice and Planning site:

### Teaching Your Children about Wealth

*Open communication, philanthropic goals and ongoing family meetings can help prepare your children to be good financial stewards.*

Similarly, Wachovia's elite Calibre unit now lists expertise on "Family Dynamics" as part of their service array to their wealthiest family clients, something unthinkable a few years back. Their family dynamics practice:

- Provides consultation on family issues to relationship teams.
- Offers direct service to client families (e.g., facilitating family meetings).
- Hosts client educational forums.
- Coordinates outside professional resources—everything from psychologists to family historians—for specialized work with clients.[2]

You also know family financial dynamics train has left the station by the time these themes are manifesting themselves in popular culture. Only in this environment could we see financial planners coproduce a big-screen movie—as they did with *The Ultimate Gift,* starring Brian Dennehy, James Garner, and Abigail Breslin—where themes of succession, inheritance, and values drive the core plotlines. Equally, the character Nick George on ABC's *Dirty Sexy Money* mounts a comic mirror to challenges advisors face in working with wealthy families. Ubiquitous, prime-time advertising, such as UBS's "You and Us" campaign is similarly feeding on and generating the powerful market sentiment that financial advisors are prepared to be far more than simply product salesmen.

So how did we get here? Among the structural drivers are the demographics of aging in baby-boom client segments and the staggering wealth transfer between generations, whose amounts are described in the trillions of dollars. Because of America's deeply ambivalent relationship to inherited wealth, these large-scale trends translate down to very personal, very complex decisions that are being guided by battalions of financial advisors who are struggling to keep up with the hype and promise of their role as family educators and facilitators.

The gap between the gathering expectation advisors and their clients are setting and the realities of everyday practice needs to be closed. Even as virtually every major wealth management organization will offer to facilitate family meetings to discuss a range of family and financial issues, from governance to education of the next generation, individual advisors asked to deliver on this promise are often unsure how to proceed.

Other drivers of this new phenomenon are many and varied, but are at the core related to the following trends:

- The commoditization of financial products has forced advisors to differentiate themselves on the basis of service, and the nature of this service involves tangling with increasingly private financial matters having high emotional valences.
- High-net-worth clients—the grail of the industry—are difficult to engage and easy to lose, placing pressure on advisors to deepen relationships on a basis different than product performance.
- Other surrounding experts, such as psychologists, physicians, and priests, are ill-equipped to deal with money topics even though they come up regularly in the course of their work.
- The expertise of other advisors (attorneys, shrinks) is often consumed reactively or as a last resort, whereas financial advisors are often engaged early—and with little or no associated stigma—during developmental or transitional times. This opens vast potential to operate proactively on issues before they escalate. But the opposite is also true. Because they are there early, unskilled financial advisors can also inadvertently throw gasoline on the fire—and many do.
- No longer a sideline discipline, behavioral economics—the science of how we unconsciously play games with ourselves regarding money—has now taken center stage, with the awarding of the Nobel Prize in economics to psychologist Daniel Kahneman. The findings from this research begin to account for a large number of previously unexplained anomalies that occur when you think humans ought to behave rationally around money. The issues are far from simply academic, however. What to do about it for those in the trenches helping people with their financial lives represents a new practice frontier for financial advisors of all kinds.

This new role advisors play—part priest, part psychologist, part coach—affects everything, from how to communicate with clients, facilitate family meetings, team up with the family's other advisors and structure wealth transfer strategies themselves, to how you attract new business and get fairly compensated for the work that gets done.

Using this practical book, you will develop the vocabulary and tools to face and embrace the new role you find yourself in—and profit from it. Drawing on existing research and interviews with leading advisors at the top of their game, this book brings together the issues, tools, and techniques advisors can use to grow their businesses in a satisfying and responsible way in this new milieu.

Your needs as an advisor have not been well met in this regard. On the one hand, the how to get rich, stay rich, plan better, or go into real estate literature provides education of the general public. Many of these books smuggle in puritanical values surrounding spending, saving, and investing, and give tools to consumers of financial services. They target an anxious consumer facing life transitions and/or financial challenges related in many cases to lifestyle maintenance through extended periods of retirement. While they don't necessarily direct their reader to their financial provider as the new high priest of lifestyle and legacy planning, they do prime the pump for those who are poised to assume the role.

This book is more about what financial advisors can do. It is here to help you step confidently into the new role as family consigliore. It will help you close the gap between the consuming public's need for life solutions—often supported by financial interventions—and the lack of preparation many advisors have had to deliver against this new demand.

Part One of this book (Chapters 1 through 3) provides background information on why we, as financial advisors, are in this position; what the risks and opportunities are; and some of the key research findings on the psychology of money and wealth.

Chapter 1 begins by charting the challenges and opportunities you face as your role shifts in the new competitive environment. This new practice terrain is laden with risks, to be sure. But it is also pregnant with opportunity to generate tremendous value for clients. The need for sound advice over differentiated products has never been stronger. As this book is being written, the subprime mortgage debacle has, among other things, shown the danger of pushing products over supporting wise choices.

Chapter 2 provides you with an executive briefing on what is known of the emerging psychology of money and wealth. The focus here is to digest key findings that can have palpable value for you in interfacing with client systems. This chapter will guide you through the new practice landscape and begin to explain why you are seeing certain behavior and events in your dealings with clients.

The premise and message of Chapter 3 is simple: You are the most valuable "instrument" in the advice-delivery system and, as such, the instrument in most need to be revisited and perfected in a new light is you. While no simple discourse on knowing oneself can capture all that is involved, the focus here is on those elements of an advisor that are within range of examination and development, including getting an understanding of the perspectives and biases you may bring to any discussion of money with families.

Part Two of the book builds on prior chapters with an emphasis on implications for the service and business models you need to consider in managing clients. Because the complexity factor has gone up rather than down, the nature of what you do and how you make money without getting bogged down in familial sand traps becomes paramount. The chapters in this part concentrate on providing a range of pragmatic tools and approaches to delivery advisory services across a range of circumstances.

Chapter 4 takes on the key fears advisors and managers of advisors have in this new environment by examining elements of a service model that takes into account how you profitably provide service to families in a more solution-driven versus product-driven environment. A new social contract between advisor and client needs to factor in this change in order for expectations to be met on both sides.

Because family meetings have figured so prominently in the new wealth management landscape, Chapter 5 goes beyond the hype to help advisors deploy different kinds of family meetings that meet particular objectives in the context of the broader service model for clients.

Chapter 6, in turn, helps advisors face down a range of life events that often figure prominently in financial decisions for clients and to be of some help—or at least do no harm. Understanding the convergences and divergences of family and financial processes in the circumstances of anticipated and unanticipated (crisis) life events can mean the difference between being very helpful or very destructive to clients.

Chapter 7 is provided to address the context in which the delivery of advice is facilitated. Advisors have various attachments to financial institutions, broker/dealers, and platform providers of many stripes. This chapter is meant to provide guidance to these entities in their efforts to reform the ways in which they support the delivery of advice and solution-centric services. In a word, what do advisors need to operate in this new environment?

Chapter 8 discusses the skills needed to augment what you already bring to the table and suggests some ways to get trained in new methods of interacting with clients.

Like other elements that have changed, ethical issues that attend this new role go beyond sales and product-specific constructs to those that take into account new responsibilities with expanded stakeholders. Using case material, Chapter 9 puts forward additional considerations when family financial interventions of the increasingly common kind are undertaken.

Two appendices provide advisors with a listing of tools that have been used in engaging client families (Appendix A) and further resources and training available for advisors.

In sum, this book represents both a call to action and a road map that can provide directional guidance for advisors. Five to 10 years ago, when products were becoming commoditized, the idea of tangling in a serious way with family dynamics was an interesting but highly localized construct in the minds and practices of some early pioneers. As with rogue waves, there were unconnected and apparently random bursts of energy and enthusiasm for work on the exotic beachhead where family and money meet. Today, surf's up and you're going to need a board to ride the wave. This book will help you take the skills you have and figure out the kind of board you will need in your specific circumstances.

Another way to look at this is the difference between changes in the weather and climate changes. As with the weather, there are daily and weekly changes in the delivery of financial services. Several seminars here and there reminding advisors and relationship managers that family dynamics matter have provided periodic, tactical gusts of information and brief storms of interest in this new domain. It is my opinion, however, that we have reached a kind of tipping point that renders visible climate-level changes in the business of embedding financial services more profoundly in the lives of clients. No longer the province of a few pioneers and gurus, this climate change is about you and what you need to better do what you are already doing: creating positive changes in the lives of your clients.

# CHAPTER 1

# Accepting the Challenge

If you're still reading this, you have accepted the basic premise that things are moving in a direction presenting you with a new mandate around working with clients. You already have a great deal of expertise and have been successful to date, and now understand that, whether you like it or not, the impact of your advice, wealth strategies, and interventions on families is substantial. As with any change that is both this subtle and this profound, there is both opportunity and risk facing you as you vector between the rock of what you know and the hard place of stepping into unknown territory. Start first by not being too hard on yourself about having trepidation about this. In fact, if what is proposed here doesn't make you nervous, there's something wrong. You have been extended an invitation to a protracted event in which the rules are still getting invented and from which there is no graceful exit.

The purpose of this chapter is to frame the challenge of the new financial advisor as someone on the frontier of change in the lives of families. The industry is changing in ways that present the advisor with risks to be managed and opportunities to capture. As such, this chapter examines the new basis of competition for the new financial advisor as it shifts toward personal solution development and away from product differentiation. We then look at the risks and opportunities present in this changing environment and conclude with some tips and takeaways regarding the work that lies ahead.

## A New Basis of Competition

As advisory business models are shifting from a commission to a fee basis, several things have happened. On the one hand, there has been a movement away from transaction-based client interactions (with minimal intimacy) toward a much more intimate client/advisor relationship where the client's financial *and* personal needs must be understood. As such, it is no longer sufficient for advisors to compete on product or price. Rather, it has become important to embed products into solutions that require advice and coordination of other components, sometimes over extended time frames.

For example, investment policy and implementation in a trust may have to be revisited regularly in the context of making sure a family rift does not emerge between the shifting current and prospective needs of income versus remainderman beneficiaries. This need to connect products and advice to living solutions for different individuals in families has not been felt or acted upon everywhere in the industry in the same way. I can walk between two advisors' offices in midtown Manhattan and talk to one advisor with $500 million under management and 1,500 clients, and another with a $1 billion under management with 50 clients. The frantic nature of the former means that our half-hour meeting is interrupted four times by four different clients who have four different financial questions that pertain to their financial needs: "Should I short this stock?" "Did we hang on to that stock too long?" "What do you think the Fed is going to do?" And the like. The same half hour spent with the latter is, by contrast, contemplative, bordering on serene. Both will say they do in-depth planning and 360-degree wealth management. Both have shifted to fee-based compensation. And while the dynamics of their businesses are different, they both say that the need to be more client intimate has gone past being desirable to forming their very basis of competition.

On the other hand, with the rise of the asset management discipline through its own maturity cycle, it has also become more and more difficult to compete on product features and price. It is not that this has been entirely erased from the market, as in the case of steep hedge fund compensation that is also showing signs of pressure or, at the other end, the emergence of innovative index products challenging the concept and need for active management. What this has come to mean for advisors, though, is that there are two broad career paths that unfold along the contours shaped by a shift in the industry's structure—being a deep product expert or being a deep relationship expert. These paths should not be construed in absolute oppositional terms, as will be shown later when we look at the new Wealth Management Model in Chapter 8. There are certainly individuals who are good at both.

The problem is in a more direct way related to the paths that organizations have to choose as they examine the true basis of their competitive advantage. The organizational correlate is the organization that gets good at being a component player in the wealth management delivery system versus the organization that concentrates on the delivery of solution-centric advice. The former has deep silo expertise—such as doing sophisticated, concentrated securities transactions or offering complex structured products.

Their challenge is to get good at embedding their products or services into those firms who themselves excel in managing client relationships. This latter organization has developed a core competency of managing relationships, both on the demand or client side and on the supply or vendor side. Relationship management–centric organizations pride themselves increasingly on their "open product and service architectures" while component players build deep intellectual capital in essential but narrow disciplines.

As seen in Figure 1.1, the shift in the basis of competition for financial advisors presents the financial services professional with a set of both risks and opportunities that are a little like looking for steady ground during an earthquake. The key in this environment is to avoid falling into the crevasse that standing still in one's practice may create. We now turn to some of the risks that are presenting themselves to advisors.

## Risks: Getting Outflanked by Change

The greatest risks in this shaky environment stem mostly from doing things the same way. They come hardest when the advisor fails to confront the reality that there is no real turning back from the larger thrust of the industry toward solution-centric wealth management. This kind of wealth management has a strong impact on client families because it necessarily focuses on wealth's human as well as financial components. Some of the risks an advisor must manage in this context include:

1. *Your practice will become ordinary.* You need to stand out! This doesn't mean that you are the only one doing work that is more sophisticated with families. It does mean that you change in ways that leave your clients surprised at how much you really care about their lives. Alternatively, your practice will become ordinary for at least a couple of reasons. One level concerns word of mouth and the ways in which memory and peer influence work in the market. Every client of a financial advisor is asked, and likes to talk about, why their financial advisor is the best. Whether around card games or social events, clients compare and contrast everything from prices to services. Because of a psychological maneuver called "cognitive dissonance," which can be translated here to mean that "because I continue to consume this advisor's services, they must be really good," a subtle contest is often set in motion between clients to see who is getting the best services. Often, if one of these individuals is in the market for a new advisor, the first reference is to the one the other individual is using. Were you to listen in, the details of how your practice is described may surprise you in the

Product Features  Cost  Ease/Convenience  Trust/Privacy  Assurance/Advice  Experience  Outcomes

Baseline Value Creation

Personalized Value Creation

FIGURE 1.1 The Shift in the Basis of Competition for Financial Advisors.

way they distort, for example, fees and other things you think you are doing.

I was recently privy to a conversation of this kind where one client was prepared to take to the mat the idea that her advisor never charged her any fees. This was a brokerage client talking to a wrap fee client. Neither one knew exactly what the other was saying, and on some level, how they were getting charged. This may be extreme, but the risk about becoming ordinary is not that what you are doing is wrong but that what you are doing is not memorable or striking in how it resonates with your clients when you are not there. The client receiving ordinary service with only passing concern for family impact will become defensive of you—and by extension, of themselves because of their invested ego in having made a good choice—instead of deeply confident in the value that you have created together.

2. *You will keep staple clients but won't make quantum leaps.* Being unwilling to change does not mean you will immediately lose your business. There is a base client segment that in fact will be just fine with little change. They may in fact prefer that, as a wealth advisor, you stay at arm's length with respect to important family wealth outcomes. They want you in a product box and would be surprised, if not unnerved, if you stepped outside of your traditional sphere. The basis of competition for them continues to be on the basics of product and price, and the extent to which you remain competitive that way means that you will enjoy a part of your book of business that is stable. Part of the risk is that, because of that social contract, you will also be vulnerable to being outpriced and outperformed. But the other part is that you will be less likely to secure major wins with larger, more meaningful client systems. I have argued in another context[1] that financial services should look to other industries and cases—such as IBM or Sun Microsystems—where product commoditization forced industry leaders to shift from a product- to solution-based approach. The risk of not doing this in wealth management is going to lie in erosion of your book of business and the elimination of your ability to compete for larger mandates with family client systems.

3. *You will not be prepared for up-market clients who by definition have financial and familial complexity.* Many advisors clamor for fewer clients with more assets—what's not to like? But you have to be prepared to shed the transactional culture so many of us grew up in and to develop your approach to complex financial families. One way to undermine yourself here is to not recognize the impact that you can and do have with client systems only to find yourself unwittingly veering away from big jobs with lots of moving parts. You will be nervous and overly cautious the minute you smell conflict and you may not

even know consciously why this is happening. Once confident making presentations to relatively passive prospects, you have learned to talk too much and listen too little. In your rush to explain the old ways you are different, you will inadvertently convey how similar you were to the last advisor they heard. In not closing the value deficit between what couples and families really need and what most providers have to sell, you will render yourself entirely forgettable. The worst part of this is that, because much of this interplay of advisor and prospect or client is unconscious, your client will have a difficult time even identifying what wasn't quite right. We have taught clients over many years to expect little from sales and service encounters—and keep delivering on this expectation. In some cases, this will work fine, but the minute the complexity of stakeholder needs becomes clear and the possibility of conflict or the need for deep problem solving exists is the moment when how you behave will leave this client yours to keep or yours to lose.

4. *You will charge people like you always have, and continue to be defensive about fees.* Nowhere will your new approach be more evident than when you begin to use different ways of charging for new services. One uphill battle we are fighting is the effects of how well we have trained clients to expect to get a number of our services for free. As psychologist George Kelly used to say, "Today's insight is tomorrow's resistance." The wealth management analogy is that when we insisted—while the markets were roaring upward—that we would charge asset-based fees, we could count this as an insight, a simplification of pricing that would tie our success to that of our clients. So we began to give away project-based services, like estate planning reviews or financial planning, "for free." The problem, of course, came when the cross-subsidization of services became problematic when markets declined. While giving away estate planning at certain asset balances became de rigueur, the cost of doing this was recognized too late: clients now came to expect expensive services for free. In fact, when markets decline, the need for these extra services hardly declines in concert. Arguably, this is when clients are most in need and most willing to explore strategies and scenarios. Now is when they want to talk, whether about refinancing or renewed needs to get on a budget.

Of course, giving something away both devalues your work and invites more and more bottomless demands. Because much of this project work entails behind-the-scenes activity on the part of the advisor and service team, it is also kept somewhat invisible to clients, who are in turn going to wonder why they are paying you the fees they're paying anyway. The argument for active management—itself a prime rationale for charging significant fees—breaks down precisely when the markets are down and advisors are in most need of a justification of why they are charging what they are.

5. *You will leave your service model alone—and so will your clients!* Part of what is challenging about changing the depth and sophistication of your approach to clients is the understandable fear that ever greater involvement with clients will become a profit killer, that you will entangle yourself in issues you are not trained or comfortable dealing with, and that it will drag you into an abyss of work you cannot manage. And while you cannot expect to turn your wealth management practice into a "psychotherapy clinic," there are some tools and techniques for running health care–related practices that actually can be deployed in this environment (something more fully addressed in Chapter 4). This may sound a bit absurd, but consider the following:

You have a client for whom greater intimacy has meant that they seem to feel entitled to call you at all hours of the night because in fact you have become the most trusted advisor. Or you have a client who is managing a parent with deteriorating mental capacity and therefore have a situation with complex start and stop features around estate planning. These may seem like nightmare scenarios, with bottomless demands on your time. But the same is true for a psychotherapy practice, and in many cases more so because of the constraints on getting paid for this kind of work placed on providers by third-party payers, not to mention their need to have a life as well. The key here is that developing intimate relationships does not mean developing unmanaged relationships with uncompensated work—what I call *shadow work*. If you leave your service model alone *and* you expect to develop more thoughtful and intimate client relationships, you are going to be vulnerable to seeing a ballooning of shadow work—work that you have to do to retain clients that is often invisible to them and uncompensated. By contrast, development of a proactive service model that bakes in new ways to manage how you touch clients and get paid for it can bring significant results to your business. This concept is important enough to require separate treatment in Chapter 4.

6. *You will leave your technical infrastructure alone—and be crushed by the work.* Technologies—just like organizations and the disciplines underlying wealth management—have evolved around the vertical silos of work, such as financial planning, credit underwriting, portfolio management and the like. That is to say, technology development has tracked the industry silos and rendered work within them much more powerful and efficient. So what is the problem? To put it simply and perhaps state the obvious, if the nature of your work needs to change, the tools and technologies that support that work need to change as well. This is manifesting itself as a discrepancy between the actual work an advisor

does and the business processes supported by the technologies advisors are required to buy or inherit from sponsors. All the good technology news has been about the vertical systems, which have made extraordinary things possible at the fingertips of advisors. The bad news is that many of the "software suites"—whether integrated or not—continue to lack functionality that supports the new way advisors work. The starkest example of this is around the palpable lack of project management functionality being developed adjacent to core applications. Most client relationship management (CRM) platforms are as bereft of this functionality as planning or portfolio systems.

The new platform for advisors needs to support horizontal management activities. It needs to help advisors manage lists and generate alerts; it needs to listen to other systems for relevant data and screen out the noise in a way that is now possible with "service-oriented architectures." It needs to track time and calculate profitability. It needs to support collaboration inside and outside firewalls. It also needs to extend itself in thoughtful and nonintrusive ways to clients and provide increasing ways to render shadow work visible. The question from clients as to why they are continuing to pay these high fees begins to vanish from the vernacular as the nature and value of work an advisor does is expressed in brilliant sight lines into what it takes to do wealth management.

## Opportunities: Getting to the Next Level with Clients

Just as there are risks in keeping your way of doing business status quo, there are major opportunities to be found in getting more adept at working in new ways with clients and their families. The new financial advisor can step into major service gaps in the wealth management industry, including the one that exists between organizations that say they are all about the lives of their clients and what they actually continue to do day in and day out. Some of these opportunities for the new financial advisor are developed below.

1. *You will genuinely "get" what your clients need, and they will know and value this.* With a greater understanding of psychological and family dynamics, a financial advisor will develop a larger appreciation of the different forms of logic that come into play when clients make high-stakes financial decisions. Why doesn't the individual who just sold their business to a publicly traded company want to diversify out of the stock? What is in the way of the execution of a brilliantly conceived estate plan? Of course, in general: Why don't clients just listen to your immaculate

financial reasoning? Climbing the learning curve here will not only help you demystify what clients are doing, it will enable you to intervene in ways that produce more durable solutions and deeper relationships with your clients. A subtle shift will begin to take place, where you move out of "convincing" and "sales" modes and into consultative and joint problem-solving modes with clients. You will collaboratively weigh the full complexity—human and otherwise—of making key decisions while conveying a palpable sense of empathy, that you really do understand what is going on and what the stakes are for them holistically. You will discover that, for example, paradoxical interventions—where you virtually talk someone out of something they should do—can have the effect of helping someone consider how odd their position is without blame or defensiveness. You will learn that tactical use of silence can say well more about how deeply you are listening than all the chatter you can muster about how the solution you propose can benefit the client. You will also learn that an empathetic statement about the difficulty of raising the client's child or the ambivalence you hear about a client's initiating divorce can carry far more force than beating quarterly benchmarks by an aggregate of 200 basis points ever will.

This is not rocket science. And it is not about turning you into a therapist. It involves rethinking the real business you're in and retooling yourself and your practice to genuinely be in that business and be strong and confident. The financial value you provide will go up and down. It is the value you provide in achieving life outcomes that will really pay the dividend.

2. *Your close and implementation rates will increase.* Estate planners know this well: they know that the actual close rates on estate planning—defined as executed documents and funded vehicles—are poor. In case after case, the difficulty around getting clients to execute wealth strategies lies in giving inadequate consideration to the larger force field in which financial decision making takes place. The reason is that this force field ebbs and flows with highly valenced familial and developmental needs, each pressing their case and presenting family leaders with dilemmas and ambivalence. And often this goes on unconsciously in the family system.

Consider the sale of a family business. The financial logic may be beyond compelling, but the impact on the vocational identity of key family stakeholders may appear virtually shattering to some and as nothing at all to others. Worries about the fate of key nonfamily employees may seem overblown to you, while providing significant employment in the community and being loyal to key people is a profound source of pride for the owners. Moreover, the financial logic notwithstanding, the owners may have different cathexes ("psychological investments") in the business, some virtually bordering on an "addiction" to the business.[2] Mom may have substantially different feelings about a sale than Dad does, each of which are still different from what the kids feel, including those that are in the business and those that are owners who are not in the business.

The point of this illustration is to suggest that because your client is the one in the room discussing options with you, and is the formal "decider" in any case, does not mean that you have dealt with the systemic forces that are in play. This is one reason you will hear the term *client systems* over and over in this book. Underexamination of the systemic and historical forces in play will place you in a persuasion or convincing mode, which will generate ambivalence in the client "decider." Then you can flip a coin—literally—to see if they take the decision you think they should. You've got about an even chance they will because instead of helping them understand the multivalenced decision field they are in, you asked them to take a position that will invariably have some form of psychological blowback. The irony here is that you will spend less time closing complex deals if you are sensitive to this than you will by ignoring what is going on in the client system.

3. *You will manage wealth, rather than just investments, and get paid for it.* Wealth management is not just investment management wrapped with some advice and planning. As I have argued elsewhere, wealth is, at the end of the day, the "ability to accomplish an outcome."[3] This means that wealth refers to the full range of human and financial assets (and liabilities) that can be organized to create an outcome. At this level, everyone has wealth—that is, an inventory of talents and capabilities as well as financial resources that can be calibrated to achieve an outcome, however modest or grand in scale. This also means that the human component cannot remain an ancillary focus of the wealth advisor's attentions. The human part cannot be perceived as an irritation in the way of growing asset balances. The physical, intellectual, psychological, and, in some cases, spiritual integrity of client systems is intimately tied up with the issues surrounding their financial integrity. This extends to the advisory team as well, which itself is often dysfunctional in its own right and one of the impediments to successful strategy execution.

The net opportunity here lies in the "management" part of wealth management. Put simply, the ability to get paid for the management of wealth and all the coordination, project management, team development, product construction, and strategy development is where the upside is for advisors who can transition their practices from product- to solution-centric enterprises. Many advisors struggle with this, and if it were easy it would not likely be as valuable to clients. But the fact remains that families need advice and strategy to accomplish objectives, and they often need it from a variety of sources. They also need management of these components through long periods of time. Step confidently into this space and you will build a very differentiable enterprise with clients who are loyal over the long term.

4. *You will see rather than ignore the effects of what you are doing and it will help you proactively spot opportunities rather than find yourself constantly in a reactive mode.* The concepts, tools, and strategies you will explore in this book are designed to help you see around the corner with respect to what your client systems need. What you will learn will also help you see the true scope of effects you are producing in your client families, some of which are unintended. No one can perfectly predict the impact of what they are going to do on even the smallest social systems. At the same time, greater awareness of your potential impact on client systems will help you bring into greater alignment the "interventions" you deploy with the outcomes that are being sought. When done with care, these interventions can continue to lay groundwork for proactive action and the discovery of new opportunities. For example, you may work with a couple to establish a budgeting regimen that you know will produce pain in one or more of the couple's children. In fact, your real objective is to shift the family economy in such a way as to align financial processes with goals that have been stated. Done with care, these steps can help you become a resource to the larger family beyond your initial client couple. Equally, the overall service model you adopt will present you with multiple points of visibility into the many moving parts of multigenerational families.

5. *You will step confidently and respectfully into a position of greater trust with your clients.* Increasing the trust quotient with clients provides undeniable opportunities for enhanced work with and revenue from clients. Working through what it means to be in the business of intervening on families—a business you are actually in anyway—will demystify aspects of what is going on between you and your clients and breathe new confidence into your work. It will not rid you of anxieties and trepidations about the work, but will instead help you face down unnecessary worries about what you are doing and transform the anxieties you do have into data needed to be more conscious of what you are doing opposite clients.

What does this mean? It means, for example, that because you are the most important instrument in the advisory encounter, if you are anxious about how a client is going to react to things you are going to say, chances are that an exploration of the basis of that anxiety will key you in to a problem with your intervention. An estate attorney once described a case in which he was about to present a client with the final drafts of a plan that called for, among other things, the creation of a family limited partnership whose interests would be held by generation-skipping trusts. On the face of it, the plan was perfect. Yet the attorney struggled with a vague sense that something was not right. He then went to another attorney who was familiar with the family and explained his unease. In the process, it emerged that there was conversational terrain that had really not been covered in the interactions with the patriarch and his wife. These issues included concepts of parenting in the couple, including what it would *mean* to their adult children (generation 2) that their children (generation 3) would stand to be substantially wealthier than their parents. The attorney in this case used his "anxiety" about what he was doing to drive a dialogue with a peer, which in turn produced a hypothesis that was worth exploring with the clients around the effects of the strategy on their children and grandchildren. This hypothesis was simply that the attorney and his client couple had not sufficiently explored the potential familial effects of what was being considered. The financial effects and benefits were clear enough; the articulation of possible family effects was needed to round out this strategy. In this case, rather than being undermined by anxiety, the attorney *used his anxiety* to speak to him about a pending client situation with high stakes. He took steps to understand its meaning and used what came out to formulate and test a hypothesis with clients. These clients, in fact, felt a tremendous relief at spending time talking about this and decided that they wanted to shift the balance of wealth to generations 2 and 3 and introduce a significant philanthropic component to alter the family wealth equation that had been previously contemplated.

6. *You may even see some clients less, but every encounter will be powerful and memorable.* How you use your time will not get any less important when you begin to rethink how you work with clients. As you get more comfortable with your new role, you will see that increased sophistication in the family intervention business does not at all mean getting vacuumed into a black hole of internecine familial warfare. In fact, thoughtful approaches to your service model will help train clients—much as they are trained in psychotherapy practices—that time counts and that there are rules of engagement that will actually enhance the quality of client encounters. Not that your quarterly investment reviews aren't the most exciting and anticipated encounters for your clients. (If that's so, they need to "get a life" anyway!) What this means is that the quality of the dialogue is going to get ratcheted up so that you will be saying less but what you do say is going to reverberate with clients and facilitate change.

7. *You will feel great about what you are doing and make more money doing it.* Dr. Keith Whitaker, head of Family Dynamics for Wachovia's elite Calibre unit—managing families with assets of $25 million and

above, spells this out perfectly, saying, "Most [of Calibre's advisors] are drawn to this work because they want to help families."[4] My experience with hundreds, if not thousands, of advisors confirms this. Many of you indeed become very drawn to this work because you are do-gooders. Some of you are closeted do-gooders and only learn of your true passion for this work over time, but it is there in your values and what you care about. The opportunity embedded in the new role change you are making is also very personal, and for many of you this turn of events in the market is going to enable you to explicitly get better than ever at changing the lives of your clients.

---

## Tips and Takeaways for the New Financial Advisor

All told, the risk and reward environment for making changes suggested in this book is very positive indeed. As you delve into the meaning and thrust of the arguments ahead, you will find that small steps can be taken in support of the reinvention of your work. The changes suggested are meant to be suggestive, directionally correct, and bite-sized. They are meant to help you think about your clients differently, elevate your skills to intervene more effectively, and do this with the support of increasingly abundant resources to help you in the cause of helping your clients realize their objectives and make money doing so.

The first tip is to open your mind to new ways of doing family wealth management. Prepare yourself for some new vocabulary that will stretch your mind. Don't use what follows as the one gospel of family wealth management; instead, take what you find useful as an invitation to elevate the dialogue in the industry and to bring your own work to the next level.

Let's now turn to the psychology of money as a way of helping you begin to understand the basics of some of the core needs and conundrums families will present to you. For many of you, this will serve as validation of your experience and provide you with a new lens through which to view issues you may have seen before but have previously stymied your work or made you want to run for the trees instead of seize them as new opportunities to grow your business.

# CHAPTER 2

# The Psychology of Money and Wealth

It usually doesn't take long in the wealth advisory business to run across client financial behavior that has you scratching your head and wondering what could possibly be motivating your clients. Many of you have seen things that no writer of fiction could make up. This chapter delves into the peculiar space where psychology and money intersect. This concept is discussed early in the book because knowing the psychology of money and wealth is a key part of being able to identify and work through a range of issues you will come across as you more intimately engage your clients in outcome-oriented value creation.

The core purpose of this chapter is not to write definitively about money behavior but to introduce a new level of curiosity and problem solving into the work that you do. As such, this chapter will familiarize you with some of the findings about the psychology of money that have practical value and foster a new way of inquiring of your clients who they are and how they think about some of the most important decisions they will make. We will examine the sources of new findings and redefine the notion of wealth and wealth management in a manner that is much more inclusive of the human context of wealth. We will also review and sensitize you to the "systems" that clients find themselves in and how that can affect their (and your) behavior. Key concepts we will review include the non-fungibility of assets and liabilities, the concept of *cathexis* and how we make psychological investments in financial and real assets, and how we often personify assets and attribute certain human characteristics to them. Finally, we will talk about the role of history and values in working with clients and conclude with some tips and takeaways for the new financial advisor.

## Sources of New Findings and Questions

Everywhere you turn, you are beginning to hear about values, family dynamics, and the psychology of money. When Daniel Kahneman, a psychologist, won the Nobel Prize in economics in 2002, what once was work of an obscure group of academics came splashing across the media as the next new paradigm for understanding financial decision making. In fact, some major research findings have been accumulating for years from academic, clinical, and commercial sources. Many of these new insights are difficult to sort through, and most advisors I know don't have the time to sift through it all. And you don't need to know it all. As such, what follows is a short course on what you need to know in your new financial advisor role.

I organize what is important in the psychology of money by tracking developments along three intellectual strands, each in various stages of development. Each of these intellectual discourses have some overlap with each other in some cases, but are distinct enough to be represented as different angles on the same kinds of challenges, namely: what makes people make the kind of financial decisions they make, particularly when an outside observer might even say these decisions are made against the individual's own interests? The discourses of behavioral economics, high-net-worth psychographic segmentation, and clinical practice each bear witness to some aspects of this question.

### Behavioral Economics

The first strand of thought touching the psychology of money involves what is variously called behavioral finance or behavioral economics. This work represents a shift in economic thinking that arose during the 1970s and 1980s to account for anomalous data emerging in dominant economic thinking. That is, economic science was unable to explain certain phenomena. Interestingly, for Kahneman, it began when he noticed and began studying common statistical errors made by expert statisticians.[1] In a nutshell, this work began to pick up speed as more and more findings began to accumulate around the basic notion that humans do not behave around numbers, money, and investing in ways that economic theory would have predicted. In the prior paradigm, this meant that something irrational was going on when it came to how people behave around money. This is nicely embodied in Belsky and Gilovich's great title on the subject, *Why Smart People Make Big Money Mistakes*.[2] However, in the emerging paradigm, the logic of how people behave around money and investing has a surprising rationality and predictability, enough so that investment managers, such as LSV Asset

Management—now with $80 billion under management—can successfully exploit behavioral tendencies using quantitative models based on the new behavioral economics. Their argument is as follows:

> *The fundamental premise on which our investment philosophy is based is that superior long-term results can be achieved by systematically exploiting the judgmental biases and behavioral weaknesses that influence the decisions of many investors. These include: the tendency to extrapolate the past too far into the future, to wrongly equate a good company with a good investment irrespective of price, to ignore statistical evidence and to develop a "mindset" about a company.*[3]

The findings from these sources are, thus, far from academic and have been shown to deeply affect both lay and professional investor behavior. The latter is something we will turn to in the next chapter. In the meantime, we will extrapolate from this emerging and compelling body of knowledge for its day-to-day significance for your work with client families.

## High-Net-Worth Psychographics and Buying Behavior

The second intellectual strand helping to clarify how people behave around money comes from marketing professionals studying issues such as investor behavior. They have concentrated on, for example, the reasons two individuals with the same amount of money to invest consume investment advisory services completely differently. Moving past the basics of demographic market understanding, these individuals have developed "psychographic" ways to characterize and typify different kinds of clients so as to more effectively sell into these segments. Perhaps emblematic of this work is Prince and File's works on cultivating the affluent, where nine profiles of affluent consumers are articulated, along with the ways of appealing to them in sales and service terms.[4]

This literature can help the advisor develop tactical means to generate greater satisfaction with services and is valuable as a result. It represents a descriptive literature that can describe how to sell and service clients but does not fully articulate the work of the advisor as acts of intervention driving toward a "greater good." For example, to get an "Innovator" or an "Investment Phobic" to buy one's services might require very different uses of investment process detail to make the sale, but not to develop wise decision making in the family system over time. Sometimes the objectives of this research can be said to be strictly commercial, though that is hardly reason to not pay attention to the many insights it has delivered.

## Findings "From the Couch"

A third and final source of insight is the small but growing literature "from the couch"—that is, the insights coming out of consulting and clinical practices of mental health professionals who have begun to gingerly step into the complications money brings into the psychotherapy process. Whether in individual, couple, or family therapy, issues of money often speak loudly and are deeply embedded in the varying psychological processes, normal and pathological, that clinicians encounter. Very few since Freud and Ferenzi have touched on the powerful way in which money is tied up in key psychological processes until recently. To some extent, this is because these professionals have just as hard a time talking about money as financial advisors have about family dynamics: the former no more chose their line of work to talk in depth about money than the latter chose high entanglements with family dynamics.[5]

John Schott's book, *Mind Over Money,* represents an important work in this literature, where he derives insight about quirks of economic behavior as both a psychiatrist/psychoanalyst and value-oriented money manager.[6] From a different angle, this work sets out less to figure out how to sell to individuals with different personalities and tendencies than it does to do the reverse: to help those with certain tendencies to counteract their impulses when those impulses can get them into trouble. So we owe to this primitive and evolving discourse the idea that, as Keith Whitaker at Wachovia has said, "everything we do [as wealth advisors] is an intervention."[7] In other words, what wealth advisors do to get the deal and keep the client needs to be understood as affecting the well-being of families, for better or worse.

As in the Heisenberg effect in physics and its analogue Hawthorne effect in social psychology, once you enter a system, even if only through observation, you change it. In wealth advising, there is no neutral ground to stand on, since even presenting a couple with two equally compelling wealth strategies creates an effect because it forces work to be carried out between the couple to make a choice. The mental health contribution thus represents the invocation of a "well-being" model into the overall discourse of wealth management. It provides an experience base that rounds out behavioral economics and psychographic market research with a well-being agenda. This enables us to derive principles from the best of each source to further family financial health.

Before turning to the core of these principles, some definitions and assumptions about wealth, wealth management, and the systems in which clients find themselves should be spelled out to clear a mind-set for what is being proposed in *The New Financial Advisor*.

## Redefining *Wealth* and *Wealth Management*

As I have alluded to earlier, wealth, the focus of our advice and products, needs to be understood as something well beyond financial assets by the new financial advisor. The etymology of the word *wealth* ties its origin to the Old English word *weal,* which refers to "the state of being well." The modern devolution of the term to connote only financial wealth is unfortunate indeed.

As in the etymology of wealth, what is being argued here is hardly original in the sense that wealth management is more like the management of "well-being" or "welfare" than, say, the management of assets or portfolios. Depending on the context, these resources can mean everything from a person's having his or her health to a society's having infrastructure and the like. Industry parlance often codes wealth with the meaning of having a certain net worth or quantity of investable assets. The wealth market ($10+ million) is often distinguished from the high-net-worth ($1 to $10 million) market and the affluent market ($500,000 to $1 million) on this basis. While segmentation of this type can be important, it turns out to be most important to the service economics of the business and less important to figuring out how you can most help the specific client in front of you.

For the "new" financial advisor and for the purpose of this book, wealth refers to the *ability to realize life goals and outcomes.* This ties the idea of wealth profoundly to the concept of well-being insofar as it integrates all forms of resources, human and otherwise. Human welfare is part of the core, not the periphery, of wealth advising. It means that client systems bring both human and financial assets and liabilities to the table with them. For the new wealth advisor, it means you have to tangle with both.

The intertwined nature of human and financial wealth can be demonstrated by looking at what happens in the negative, as when there is a degradation of the human "assets." Examples of this may include a disabled soldier returning from overseas combat to a ruined career; an entertainer broken by drug addiction; or a family business foundering in the hands of an underqualified blood successor.

## Clients Are Part of Systems

The idea that clients are part of family and other systems may seem to be a truism to some and inscrutable to others. For our purposes, the important sense to be conveyed is that even if you are talking to a client one-on-one for a long period of time, it is easy to forget that they participate in a number of sociotechnical systems and a problem to act as if they don't have an impact on client issues and decision-making. These systems can include:

- *Society.* Society includes the culture—that dense and highly intractable system of meaning deeply tied to language—and other social, legal, and economic systems having their own impact on what is normal and pathological with respect to money and wealth.
- *Family.* Everyone I know came from a family and received some of their deepest instruction about money—consciously or not—in this environment they did not choose and over which they exercised limited control. Often, they are in families of their own making and these individuals are not neutral players as regards the flow and management of wealth in its various forms.
- *Work.* As will be discussed in more detail later, one's relationship to the production of wealth or its consumption can have a pervasive impact on how wealth resonates in the individual and his or her overall relationship to wealth around whether it is experienced as a product of one's own efforts (e.g., Oprah Winfrey), an accident of birth (e.g., Paris Hilton) or dumb luck (e.g., lottery winners).

This concept of systems is primitive and not at all presumed to be exhaustive. The implication for day-to-day practice, however, ties directly to the quality of conversations you are able to establish with your clients. In this process, being able to identify the "voice" you are hearing from clients around financial matters provides an important inroad into the deeper tentacles of meaning tied to money and wealth. These systems often make their most personal manifestation in clients as voices—not hallucinations per se in most cases, but rather coded messages speaking through the client simply because they are members of these systems. In your mind, and eventually with your client, you can really deepen your understanding of your clients by thoroughly listening and later identifying the nature of a client's participation in a particular system. In order to do so, you may ask yourself: Whose voice am I really hearing during this conversation about money? Is this their father talking, their mother? Is it the voice of a peer group (e.g., "rich guys") that represents a particular way one is supposed to relate to and behave around substantial financial resources? What is really being said? What assumptions are being carried as if they were written in stone? Are there tinges of guilt or remorse in what is being said? If so, can we track their origin and understand if they are helping or hindering what the client is trying to do?

The bottom line is, as an advisor, I do not have the power to extricate individuals from their embeddedness in powerful systems that operate on all of us in ways that are primarily out of conscious control. Systems like this also resist simple reasoning when you are trying to alter them. You cannot reason your father's voice out of your head any easier than you can simply decide to "fire" your family and all of their historic influence. Systems like these often require thoughtful and sustained interventions over significant periods of time.

With these definitions and assumptions in place, we now turn to some of the key findings regarding the psychology of money that seem to operate at the bedrock level of what advisors need to know. In many cases, the discussion to come will reinforce things you have already come to know about the work. It should also prompt you to consider different forms of intervention when encountering complicated family wealth challenges.

## The Nonfungibility of Assets and Liabilities—Financial and Human

As many advisors know from experience, all forms of money and wealth are not equivalent. One cannot pay one's utility bill with one's watch, even though they are of roughly the same value. This apparently obvious principle is one of the most important constructs operative in conversations about wealth at every level. Related to the idea of "mental accounting" put forward by behavioral economists, this principle states that money assigned to different mental buckets is not substitutable.[8] All you really need to do to understand this concept is to imagine asking a client for a $1,000 financial planning fee, knowing that they have several different sources to draw from, including:

- Their own checking account.
- A 401k retirement account.
- They could sell their house or a car.
- They could ask a spouse for it (after all, in most states, what's mine is yours as a spouse anyway).
- They could sell publicly traded shares in a trust account of the family company founded by their recently deceased father.
- They could get it from settlement money surrounding the death of their child on September 11, 2001.

It is not hard to imagine which of these sources are more likely to be drawn down for your fee. If all these potential sources of cash to meet your fee were fungible, they would be equivalent sources of cash. But we know they are not. Even when they are equally liquid, they are not equivalent in spite of their economically equivalent value.

Therefore, this notion of mental accounting turns out to have a double edge to it. On the one hand, relabeling and sequestering assets in different mental buckets can promote savings behavior against the propensity to overconsume resources.[9] The genius of this can be found in the investment industry's success in lobbying for tax-deferred retirement accounts, buckets of money proving to be highly resistant to being raided by their owners. On the other hand, sometimes these mental buckets can create illusions that one is saving more and consuming less than one believes.

One downside of this mental accounting can be illustrated in an example related to mental accounting on the basis of the size of transactions articulated below by Gary Belsky and Thomas Gilovich in *Why Smart People Make Big Money Mistakes*. They instruct the reader to review the following two scenarios:

> **Scenario 1:** *Imagine that you go to a store to by a lamp, which sells for $100. At the store you discover that the same lamp is on sale for $75 at a branch of the store five blocks away. Do you go to the other branch to get the lower price?*

> **Scenario 2:** *Now imagine that you go to the same store to buy a dining room set, which sells for $1,775. At the store you discover that you can buy the same table and chairs for $1,750 at a branch of the store five blocks away. Do you go to the other branch to get the lower price?[10]*

Time and again, the research shows that more people will go to the other branch in the first case but not the second. The same amount of money is at stake, but the relative size of the transaction creates a different sensibility in the consumer. This translates to a problem financial planners see all the time: people don't make their savings objectives because it is often in the small transactions of a meal out here or a DVD bought there that the budget is blown.

In addition, one can go the other way and be financially eclipsed by creating buckets and assigning them to overly conservative processes, such as putting an inheritance in a bank account paying 3 percent because it would be too emotionally devastating to lose the corpus of this very personal money by investing in riskier securities.[11] The fact of erosion by inflation does not enter into this kind of thinking and can significantly degrade the financial value of this money.

There are scores of studies that back up the notion that meanings assigned to segregated portions of wealth have profound effects on how people behave around money and play tricks on themselves. We cannot look at all of them here, but we can say that a key thing you must do when getting to know your clients is to listen deeply to the ways in which mental accounting is going on in your client system. And using the idea of client system deliberately shows why this is complicated, for it is one thing to understand the mental accounting of one individual and quite another to understand those processes among an interlocking set of stakeholders, such as a spouse, children, or members of your extended family with whom you have financial ties. This concept is particularly poignant in work with business owners, where there may be a range of family and nonfamily stakeholders having more than a passing interest in your deliberations about succession planning.

At the simplest level, many couples whose "charts of mental accounts" are dissimilar often find themselves in serious trouble as they become polarized around spending and saving. In one couple, the husband made the bulk of the money but outsourced all the bill paying to the wife. She in turn was constantly frantic and irritated at his overspending. He couldn't figure out what she meant. He made a significant amount of money and couldn't understand why buying a shirt here, going out to eat there, and buying the smallest things would create such anxiety in her. It was only when she was able to sit him down and show that they were running a $250 per month deficit, in large part because of all these small transactions, that he began to mitigate the effects of small transaction size on his spending behavior. This episode also told the wife that she could no longer anesthetize her husband from the realities of what was going on by sheltering him from financial data. She could still do the bills, but they needed to meet once a month to see how they were doing.

This example also provides entrée to the concept that human assets and liabilities are often not fungible either. In the above example, the styles and capabilities of each person in the couple combined to function in ways that were suboptimal. Because he couldn't be bothered with bookkeeping, she took on the mantle of fiscal conservatism in the couple and assumed the anxiety that this generated as well.

Now imagine that the stakes are even higher, as in the case of a family business where the senior generation is contemplating a range of succession scenarios that range from transferring the business to the next generation, securing an outside controlling investor, going public, or selling the business outright. It is far from unusual to see business-owning family members placing the business itself in differing mental buckets. For some, it is an asset over which they feel the most control and are willing, as a result, to look the other way regarding its risk characteristics. For others, it is a profound source of identity and meaning. For some, it's a familial ball and chain and source of daily misery, while for still others, it's a source of cash flow. For children growing up, it can be the favored sibling dominating Dad's attention (his "baby"), while virtually being simultaneously experienced by the wife as "the other woman" on whom he dotes and with whom he spends most of his waking hours.

It is in this context of business ownership that the human components of wealth appear most intertwined with wealth. Lack of fungibility among "human assets" could hardly find a more visible manifestation when questions of family stewardship and operational expertise reveal gaps such that the family enterprise may itself move into significant jeopardy when rearranging the human players.

Interventions of the advisor in these circumstances carry many risks associated with the faulty appraisal of the "mental accounting" being carried out on the business, including blowback from:

- Siding with one faction over another, even if in subtle and unconscious ways.
- Failing to incorporate multiple perspectives related to the disposition of the business.
- Failing to view any position you take as an advisor as if there won't be resistance to you in the system.
- When encountering this resistance and being defensive about it instead of seeing it as inevitable and creating the conditions in which the family can work it through.

Thus, these systems are emblematic of the ways in which:

- The underlying security (the business itself) is viewed differently through each participant's eyes.
- The people part of the business (the human assets and their liabilities) are no more fungible than is the business with other forms of wealth.

## Cathexis: The *Psychological* Investments We Make

The notion of "cathexis" is a concept Freud used in his "economic" theory of mind to describe the ways in which individuals attach psychic energy or "libido" to an object, whether that object is an idea or a thing. While Freud's and subsequent followers' work concentrated on cathexes to body parts and representations of others such as parental figures, this concept is useful insofar as it begins to account for some of the rather complex relationships individuals have to aspects of their wealth.

We've all heard the jokes about the role sports cars, jets, and enormous houses sometimes have for their owners—and, of course, we also know how humor often provides us with clever access to a sometimes painful truth.

What is increasingly important, however, is the advisor's ability to really track the kinds of psychic investments or cathexes made to everything from individual securities and funds to business assets and real property. This is especially true under the circumstances where there is a hypercathexis, or overinvestment of libidinal energy in an asset.

In some cases, an asset in which there has been a strong cathexis dulls the owner's ability to make prudent decisions concerning the asset. One example is familiar to many advisors who have had clients who sold a business to a publicly traded company in a stock-for-stock transaction and who refuse to diversify away from the stock. One advisor described a classic case wherein a client of the firm sold a business to a public company and was resistant to putting a collar on the stock he received in exchange for his business. The lead advisor strongly recommended this strategy to diversify the risk of having one stock account for such a dominant component of the client's wealth. At the time, the stock was trading at $42 per share, and it was suggested they collar it at $45 and begin to diversify across a more balanced portfolio of stocks and bonds. The client resisted for months, claiming in part that the company itself had a sufficiently diversified product line. This way of thinking is well within bounds in one's role as a business owner, but represents a potentially destructive way of viewing one's assets after a liquidity event. The stock, in this example, did indeed rise to $65 per share, but subsequently fell to $0.50 per share when accounting irregularities were disclosed. This stock basically remained a penny stock and turned our former business owner's $30 million into virtually nothing.

Unfortunately, this story is not unique. Time and time again, businesses are sold to public companies and owners hang on to those stocks well beyond the call of reason. This represents the profound way in which someone can hypercathect to first their own business and, through a process of transference, to the second business. Advisors often see this as simply an inability to "let go," or what we would call "decathecting" from the primary business. The business owner's experience is anchored to his previous asset—his company—and he transfers this same sensibility to his new holding regardless of how many conditions have changed, not the least of which is how much control he is able to assert over the new company's well-being. In many cases, endless meetings showing the benefits of tax-sensitive stock-sale strategies and the overwhelming benefits of following a plan for diversification fall on deaf ears. On one level, the client will show interest in these strategies and will make the meetings. On another level, a profound resistance to executing the strategy dumbfounds the advisor. The client will not listen to reason, even to the point of risking their entire fortune. Both client and advisor are stumped and caught in a peculiar dance with misaligned rhythms and unsatisfying outcomes.

I believe these and like encounters where there appear to be virtually pathological attachments to assets come about as the effects of powerful cathexes that often operate outside the conscious awareness of clients—and advisors. They appear as fixations and obsessions. Sometimes they represent what psychoanalysts refer to as psychic objects around which a complex set of feelings emerges. The example of selling off a parcel of land routinely illustrates the way in which these investments—or as Olivia Boyce-Abel of Family Lands Consulting says, "unwanted emotional baggage"—can tear a family apart.[12] For one family member, the land is a candy store of pent-up cash; for another, selling it would be like "stabbing Daddy in the heart."

Psychoanalyst and money manager John Schott has tracked some of these relationships to stock holdings, and has seen patterns of personification and projection between owners and their stocks, as if stocks can care about you or punish you or make you feel better about yourself. Consider a basic premise in his work:

> *Every drive associated with money gets played out in investing—the longing for security, the guilt engendered by feelings of greed, the quest for power and esteem, the fear of being abandoned, the search for love, the dream of omnipotence. Emotions are not peripheral to the investing process—a matter of "keeping one's head" when the bull tops out or the bear roars in.* Emotions are central; they are the entire ball game. If we want to make money, we need to know the rules.[13]

Schott goes on to describe emotions in investing as the "invisible advisor" that doesn't "always act in our best interest."[14] He further reread Benjamin Graham's strategy as an effort to mitigate the effects of the "market's mood swings between mania and depression" but goes on to typify seven types of investor, to a large extent based on the form of their cathexes to stocks and sometimes to the markets in general. These include the

- I-can't-stop-worrying investor (with obsessive-compulsive tendencies).
- Power investor (overidentification with stocks and getting hurt by them).
- Inheritor (high concentrations of guilt).
- Impulsive investor (falling in and out of love with an investment).
- Gambler (traders with obsessive tendencies).
- Make-me-safe investor (search for certainty with risk aversion that gets in the way).
- Confident investor (doesn't hypercathect and does not use the market to manage psychological deficits).

The key here is to imagine the total psychological balance sheet when working with client systems. There are ways, such as Dr. Schott's or others to characterize patterns in money behavior. At the same time, because you don't always know when a cigar is just a cigar, you have to burrow into the meaning of various assets and liabilities in all their specificity for each individual to really understand both the persuasive levers to use in delivering advice and to help clients build countervailing supports to help them stay the course when emotional drivers want to supersede your advice.

## The Personification of Assets (Assets Are People, Too)

Deep listening to clients will often reveal relationships to assets and liabilities that are palpably personified. It is not unusual, for instance, to hear a client-system describe the family business as "Dad's baby" without yet consciously understanding the potential significance of this. In fact, the commonness of the metaphor may make it seem superfluous up until the moment where a sale of the business is being contemplated. It is only then that the logic of the personified asset begins to unfurl. Dad was in some fairly literal ways acting like it was his baby: he spent more time with it than any other sibling, gave it more care, allowed it to drain financial capital from the family (as the preferred sibling) in early years, and seemed on the verge of a more painful transition and loss cycle than when his "actual" children left home for college than when actually selling the business.

This example illustrates what often takes place when our cathexes take the form of interpersonal objects with anthropomorphic resonance in the wealth holder. Drawing out the example above, the mom in that situation may be like many and describe the business as more like the "other woman" for all the same reasons his children describe it at his "baby." He spends more time with her, fusses over her more, and the like.

Alternatively, some may build up relationships with individual securities and begin to feel like the stock is actually "doing something to me," as if it knows you own it or cares about you. Clients with borderline personality may cycle through holdings like they do in their volatile attachments to people. Early infatuation may be followed by disappointment and rejection, as if the stock understood the client more than their last stupefied romantic partner. Clients with bipolar tendencies may move into moods that inversely track the markets. Individuals with depressive tendencies may view downward plummeting stocks as further evidence of their inability to choose relationships well, and have these feelings laced with guilt and anger. Obsessive-compulsive individuals may require real-time Internet feeds and go through elaborate and exhausting rituals to ward off anxiety around the market's daily volatile treatment of them. For paranoid processes, persecution could come from any number of asset or market quadrants.

The fuller nature of personification and other attributions of characteristics to assets—from demonization to virtual worship—represents a new frontier for more systematic research and should be connected with behavioral finance research on mental accounting and specific issues such as loss aversion.

In this context, the role of the new financial advisor often starts to resemble that of a literary or movie critic drilling into sometimes complicated characterizations of, plots around, and roles concerning a family's assets. They have to read the client's story dispassionately and make as few assumptions as possible about how asset objects take on lives of their own and are treated as actors in the family drama. Trust officers, for example, have talked for some time about how wrapping assets up in trusts often creates another sibling in the family system—and not necessarily one endearing to the other siblings on hand. The new financial advisor's need to listen deeply and in some cases to deconstruct the narratives and performances of families and their assets can help the advisor intervene in ways that can unfreeze family financial decision making, particularly in highly valenced, risky circumstances.

## Doing History: What Goes Around Comes Around

Consistent with the idea of understanding the specifics of the psychology in play in your client systems is the critical role history plays in architecting the issues you are confronting in the present. In this context, we are in search of both the meaning of wealth and the mechanisms that are operative in client systems that often overdetermine—that is, provide multiple causes of—client behavior in relation to money and wealth.

The first pass at history, familiar to most advisors, is to identify and discuss the source of the wealth. In their recent article, "Acquirers' and Inheritors' Dilemma: Discovering Life Purpose and Building Personal Identity in the Presence of Wealth," Dennis Jaffe and James Grubman have recently summarized the dynamics often attending a range of situations regarding the acquisition and/or inheritance of wealth.[15] They relate these dynamics to key sources of wealth:

- Financial windfall by effort (sale of a business).
- Financial windfall without effort (fortunate events, such as winning the lottery or through celebrity or athletic ability, or inheritance).
- Financial windfall without effort (negative events, such as sudden or complicated bereavement or litigation).
- Inherited wealth (from birth versus inheriting it during adulthood).

Each of these situations can have a profound impact on one's identity and consequently one's financial outlook. In each situation in which there is a financial windfall, it is not enough to know that it is very different in getting the money via one's own efforts versus through luck or happenstance that is either positive or negative. These authors describe wealth acquirers as going through a "psychological and sociological sensation of *transition*. The individual achieving wealth status travels not across distance but across socioeconomic class, setting out from blue-collar or middle-class culture toward the promised land of wealth."[16] Key to this sense of transition is the fact that "these individuals come to their new status having already developed much of their personal identity in the economic culture of their birth."[17] This is very different from inheritors of multigenerational wealth who are "natives of the land of wealth" where the wealth preexists the individual and can be part of delays in emotional development, motivational problems, inadequate self-esteem, guilt, social alienation, and suspiciousness of others.

Using our broadened definition of wealth means that one does not have to have large amounts of wealth for these dynamics to be relevant, nor is the need to do history obviated. If wealth is human and financial, it does not only matter in what quantity it arrives: it is still historical and should be examined as such whether there is an experience of abundance or lack.

As a new financial advisor, doing this history should not simply be a matter of checking a box regarding the source of wealth. Rather, inviting clients to tell it as a story will heighten the nuances of plot and character development that you are interested in using to deepen your understanding of the client system. It will add color to the portrait you are trying to paint of not only the individuals before you but the other players in the lives of your clients.

Several experts have adopted the use of financial genograms to help provide structure to this inquiry. This technique, derived from family therapy, provides a way to lace together the family part of the story by developing family trees that include financial information. A simplified version of this can be found in Figure 2.1 and illustrates how it is possible to gain significant insight into current conundrums by looking back a couple of generations.

The couple illustrated in Figure 2.1, Philip and Jeanie, were reasonably financially secure by most standards until Philip, a family physician, was involved in a car accident that prevented him from continuing to practice medicine. Jeanie was diagnosed with multiple sclerosis as well and similarly could no longer work. This led to a substantial financial crisis, because neither had large savings because both had been through previous divorces and had been substantially stripped of large portions of their savings in the process. However, they were anticipating receipt of a substantial, seven-figure settlement related to the accident.

Their problem, however, was just as much a function of the process by which they made decisions as it was the near catastrophic loss of financial resources. Even with the coming arrival of substantial assets, they were

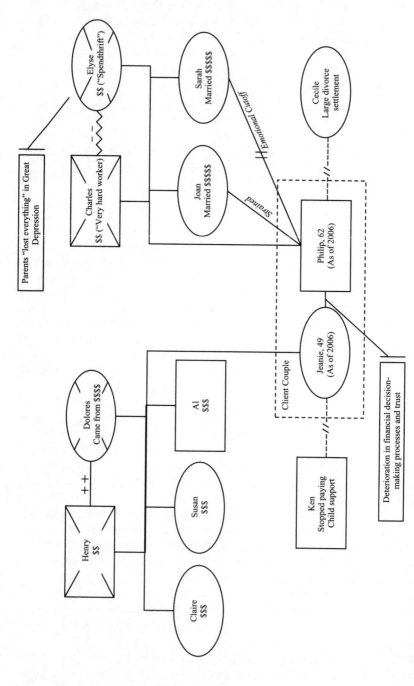

**FIGURE 2.1** Partial Financial Genogram of Philip and Jeanie.

constantly fighting. Being at home all day together, under highly deprived circumstances, had led to painful bickering and mounting mistrust. A simple genogram provided the couple with the historical backcloth informing current interactions around money and helped them begin the process of changing how the next chapter in their story as a couple would be written instead of simply acting out old familial scripts. It also surfaced current antagonisms aggravating sibling conflict around money matters that were spilling over into family gatherings. It also indicated on Philip's side an intergenerational pattern of "women spending the hard-won wealth" of the men, something that superheated his current relationship with Jeanie even though Jeanie was clearly the object of projection and did not feel that she "deserved" this fabrication of her role in the marriage.

This and other techniques help tease out the messaging about money, self, and work that form the basis of taken-for-granted assumptions about wealth. Often, asking clients to simply describe two or three messages they got from each parent about money can provide introductory access to how money and wealth are viewed, as well as frame potential conflicts in current relationships that are driven by deep assumptions baked in each person's psyche from childhood. But these messages are abundant in the culture as well, making them as intransigent as those learned from parents and grandparents. One only needs to look at home ownership—the "American dream"—as a nexus of messages that emanate from everywhere and support deeply held forms of mental accounting about the role of a house in the mental economy of the family. None other than banking mouthpiece Alan Greenspan articulates what everyone has had drummed in, namely, that home ownership is practically sacred in our culture.[18] This happens even as other voices, like Robert Kiyosaki, quietly remind us that, in fact, our houses are typically held as assets on the bank's balance sheet, not our own.[19]

## The Role of Values

Values are deeply related to the notion of wealth. Values in this sense are expressed by where people invest their time, energy, and money. They do not float in some semi-important region of mental life, but are always concretized by these investments. There is, thus, never a time when I am not expressing my values, since even sitting idly on a beach is an investment of time and probably money.

From a retrospective point of view, one's values can always be abstracted from behavior. Prospectively, there can be more or less frequent discrepancies between what I might say my values are and what I actually do. In financial terms, I might imagine myself as someone who fosters independence of action in my children only to find that I have systematically, if unconsciously, instructed my estate planner to build out incentive trusts that are virtually guaranteed to infantilize my children for decades. I can kid myself that I am charitably inclined as a way of masking a near constitutional hatred of paying taxes. I can stand on a soapbox bemoaning the decline of democracy but run my family business like a dictatorial strongman.

At the same time, this apparently ephemeral construct called values is not as relative at the individual level. Values form such a core of *who* we are as people that to rob a person of their core values is to strip them of their identity. If someone has a deep value of freedom and that is taken away, they are changed in a way that would be less so for someone who values justice.

For the financial advisor, the slippery construct of values presents a challenge. On the one hand, advisors know that if they promote a decision that flies in the face of a person's values, they run the risk of having the solution bounce off. On the other hand, how does one really get to the bottom of another's values if they are so difficult to genuinely and truthfully identify? Scott Fithian, in his book *Values-Based Estate Planning,* is among several who have taken up this challenge. Scott's company, The Legacy Companies, which is now managed by his brother Todd Fithian, is among companies that have built tools to evolve the way personal values can be tapped to more squarely drive financial decision making. One thing they promote is the assessment and comparison of both members of a couple in order to look for differences and convergences in prospective values. My belief is that the short answer on how to assess core values is to combine retrospective (what did you actually do) with prospective (what do you think you would do) assessments, and begin looking for discrepancies.

We will turn back to values at various junctures. But for now the new financial advisor needs to identify and work with whatever tools enable them to operate within the value systems of clients. Values are ignored at the peril of the advisor's relationship to the family, as can be seen time and again when they were ignored in the construction of estate plans, the plans that don't get executed.

## Tips and Takeaways for the New Financial Advisor

We have not by any means exhausted the range of issues and patterns driving the wealth psychology of your clients. The key things to remember can be summed up as follows:

- Deep listening to your clients will help you understand the *lack of asset fungibility* in your clients and begin to drive awareness between you and your clients about the *processes of mental accounting* that may be driving their behavior outside conscious awareness.

- Once these processes begin to surface, they can be broken down into the *types of cathexes* operating with respect to the psychic projections and investments (together with psychological "return" expectations) being made into various components of the family's balance sheet. These will help you map the mental money landscape into which you are treading, and warn you of "sacred cows," whose position in the minds of your clients needs flushing out. Knowing that you are working with a client system having multiple cathexes to the same objects will help you understand any fields that are mined and begin to suggest the tools for disarming them.
- Similarly, you will find in listening to your clients that certain assets may play personified roles in the wealth narrative being spun by your clients. Keeping in mind that a given asset can play different roles for different participants of the family system will be key in understanding potential flash points in family relations and wealth strategies.
- When in doubt, do the history of the present by either means of financial genograms or other conversational methods to understand the story that has been told and is being written. Knowing that there are sometimes multiple narratives—each with their own characters, plots, lead-ins, climaxes, and endings—can help you and your clients flag new areas of choice and begin the writing of the "next chapter" of their lives.
- Out of history comes values, the guiding principles that manifest themselves in how your clients invest time, energy, and money. Tracking value discrepancies—within an individual and between client system stakeholders—provides a window into the deeper needs of your clients and ways in which some strategies will be more adoptable than others when everything else is equal.

We will turn to further examples to help you understand how this plays out in subsequent chapters.

# CHAPTER 3

# Know Yourself

Until now, we have concentrated on market and research factors setting the stage for your evolving work with clients. We now turn to the most valuable asset you have at your disposal: yourself. More than any other tool, you are the instrument that will deliver the most profound effects in client systems. This means you have to know yourself—what drives you and how you are reacting in the moment to the range of issues clients will present. Learning how to understand and work with how you react in different situations will be one of the most important things you develop over time. The journey you commence here will perfect insights you have about yourself and the work you do day in and day out with clients. It will ground you more as a person, even as it expands your repertoire for dealing with complex financial families.

The purpose of this chapter is to serve as a launching pad for greater self-knowledge. By better knowing yourself, you increase the chances of being able to get out of your own way when it comes to working with families. For many, knowing yourself better is valuable in its own right. I am concentrating here, however, on the very practical problems that can arise as you engage the broader dimensions of wealth in your client systems. We will look specifically at blind spots advisors sometimes have and borrow the notions of transference and countertransference from psychoanalysis to help inform advisors on their journey for greater self-knowledge. We will also examine interpersonal communications training as a basic component of the work, along with a framework for doing peer supervision—another construct that can be productively borrowed from the mental health training community and deployed by the new financial advisor in support of greater self-knowledge and more effective practice.

## How Blind Spots about Yourself Can Get in the Way: A Case in Point

Knowing yourself better is more than an ephemeral concern in the new frontiers of family wealth management. We all have blind spots about ourselves, and some are more lethal to the work we do than others—and it is those blind spots that are (1) within reach for most advisors to uncover and (2) stand to most get in the way of what we do to which we turn now.

Consider the case of an advisor who was working with a father and son working together in a business owned by the father. Succession discussions had begun to emerge between the father and son, and the advisor—trusted over many years regarding the financial affairs of the father—was asked to facilitate discussions that included the usual range of topics, from how the father would retire and pass shares of the business to whether the son was up to taking on the mantle of the business. The more the discussion trailed on, however, the more aggravated the advisor became with the father. The advisor increasingly found the father to be excessively intransigent around his financial requirements in retirement, and was particularly peeved when the father would threaten to sell the business out from under the son because of the latter's lack of ability to step into the role of president effectively. During one meeting, the advisor's frustration came to a head. He had found himself defending the son's buyout proposal only to find both the father and son turning on him with uncharacteristically raised voices. The son even began to lead the attack, saying the advisor had crossed the line in being so argumentative with his father.

Debriefing the advisor around this escalating conflict revealed that seven years prior to this episode, the advisor had found himself in a similar situation with his own father, and it had ended badly, with the advisor leaving the business and becoming estranged from his father. As is often the case subsequent to painful situations like this, the advisor unconsciously projected himself into the current situation in a manner that would allow him to vicariously repair damage from his earlier crisis. He had accepted the facilitation role between father and son in part to do this, to repeat and repair an old wound. This is hardly abnormal or pathological. As historical beings, we draw all experience from the past and use it to drive into and make sense of the present.

Where this became problematic was at the point where the advisor lost his *orthogonality* or neutrality opposite his client system. This narrowed the advisor's ability to bring distance and perspective to the embattled dyad. This growing blind spot set the stage for the biggest surprise to the advisor: that the son, on whose behalf he believed he was operating, in fact really did want to get out of the business and had little confidence in his own ability to run it in his father's absence. The son's own ambivalent feelings about coming out with this ended up driving him to defend himself against what he saw as an increasingly belligerent approach to the father being taken by the advisor. The son—in order to avoid the direct revelation of his fears to his father—consistently fielded transfer scenarios he knew deep down the father wouldn't accept. It was easier for him to back the father into an exit strategy involving a sale of the business than to have it seem as if this result were the effect of the son's not being able to take on the leadership challenge of running the business. The advisor was unconsciously perceived by the son as blocking his exit from the business and his buried wish that the father would in fact sell the business.

## All Too Human Advisors

While this may seem to be an extreme example, in reality, these mechanisms of projection and cross-identification make up the fabric of everyday life. Happily, where there are methodologies in place to review these reactions to client systems, these responses can actually become tools for expanding rather than contracting your understanding of client systems. We will return to this concept later in the chapter when we discuss the role of peer supervision in your evolving practice.

The quest to know yourself is far from simple, but there are basic ways in which this can be undertaken. For starters, there is need to embrace the principle of *reflexivity* with respect to the arguments of the last chapter concerning the mental games we can play with ourselves around money and wealth. Reflexivity in the social sciences means that if a principle can be said to apply to human beings broadly, then it also applies to the expert who developed the principle. In other words, advisors are subject to the same forces at work around the psychology of money and wealth as are their lay clients. Recall that part of the foundation of behavioral economics was built on observations of the statistical blind spots of statisticians. This is also the case for advisors and their relationships to all forms of wealth.

Therefore, you can begin the process of understanding yourself by looking, for example, at the system and society in which you participate, your own historical and familial development around money, and the means by which your mental accounting and object cathexes to different forms of wealth came to partly make who you are and what you believe.

Debates around estate taxes can serve as an example of a social issue about which each advisor has a point of view. Our society is very ambivalent about whether meritocracy should rule and everyone should be born with an equal opportunity to make something of themselves or whether estate taxation should be eliminated to facilitate the passage of wealth along bloodlines. Arguably, the Revolutionary War was fought around the core issue as to whether wealth and power should be a matter of bloodline succession. So advisor's have to ask themselves where they stand on the matter of estate taxes, because how you are oriented to this will affect the way you assist families with intergenerational planning. It's an example of how not being completely clear on where you stand can affect in more or less subtle ways the very financial and estate strategies you support.

Yet another simple way to look at the system you are in is to examine the assumptions your business model makes about wealth. In investment-centric firms, the very definition of wealth is eclipsed to mean liquid, investable assets. Other hybrid forms of human and financial capital, such as those represented by business assets, that lie outside this view are often seen as impediments or irritations in the sales process—if they don't completely disqualify the client from the pipeline altogether. Thus, your business and service model is already supplying a kind of "mental accounting" of the client's balance sheet components. Your internalized relationship to industry vantage points will very definitely shape the work you do and are worth revisiting. For those who have strong interests in work with families, the sea in which we swim becomes part of us, for better or worse.

Further exploration suggests that the exercise, for example, of doing your own money genogram can develop another angle on the ways in which you view wealth and how it is often the product of significant events across multiple generations: the enormous success of a maternal grandfather's business, the financial devastation of a branch of the family during the Great Depression, or the radical juxtaposition of rich and poor in the same sibling group and the effects this may have had on the cousin clan.

As advisors, we are hardly immune to strong feelings and perspectives about where wealth comes from and what is done with it, nor to the various configurations of greed, fear, entitlement, or abuse that attends the flow of wealth in families. Just as there is a segment of psychotherapists and counselors who unconsciously choose their career as a process to repeat, understand, and repair familial damage, so too do many advisors choose careers that present encounters with money and wealth conundrums day in and day out.

To repeat: this is not pathological; it should be viewed as instructive and as part of what you simply need to know about yourself so as to avoid interpersonal bear traps that attend any entanglements with families and money. So every technique you might use to tease out money attitudes and values should be turned on yourself. Ask yourself what messages you got from your mother and father about money and wealth. And how did your parents get that way? What values do you have with respect to money? How should financial decisions be made? In open and democratic ways or unilaterally in a shroud of secrecy?

At the Money and Family Life Project at the Ackerman Institute for the Family, we found that work with families entails an approach to values that differentiates content values (e.g., social justice, entrepreneurship, disease eradication) from process values (e.g., inclusiveness, unilateralism, democratic). As for families, content values for you as an advisor can be articulated as well. Some methodologies for values elicitation can be found in Appendix A, and the point is that you can do these activities yourself. So, too, with process values, which describe how you make financial decisions. Using critical incident methods, you can, for example, identify that last three major financial decisions you made and review them along such lines as the extent to which you were inclusive of stakeholders versus unilateralist in your approaches.

## The Transference and Countertransference Challenge for the New Financial Advisor

The admonition to know yourself better is not always easy to take in. For one thing, the connection to how it will help you tune your practice may not seem direct. One of the more difficult concepts to grapple with is what psychoanalysts have called transference and countertransference. Transference is described in psychoanalytic terms as a substitution of feelings and reactions from one person to another. In psychoanalysis per se, it is often the case that reactions to a parental figure are transferred to the therapist. Part of the work of analysis is to deconstruct this over time. Its importance lies in helping the person doing analysis to work through impediments this transference may place in the way of having realistic and less distorted relationships with others. If I am constantly reacting to authority figures at work as if they were my stern father around whom I built many defensive maneuvers, I am not able to differentiate different kinds of authority figures and the differing styles of approach needed to work with them. In this sense, transference can get in the way of any number of potentially successful interactions.

Countertransference describes the reactions of the analyst to the patient, and has all the same potential of getting in the way of psychoanalysis. This is why psychoanalytic training requires that the psychologist or psychiatrist expecting to do psychoanalysis go through a "training analysis" themselves. An analyst has to, first, understand and, second, manage the reactions that get evoked in them. In the most basic sense, interpersonal exchanges are individuals reacting to each other's reactions. The job of the analyst is to use his or her reactions to inform his or her interventions. If the analyst is getting anxious or angry or bored, they step back and ask "what is going on here." What am I reacting to? Am I, for example, falling asleep when you talk because I'm tired or because you are using a defensive process to keep me at a distance—something that boring me will do. The analytic contract is to render all of these reactions to reactions fair game with regard to advancing the treatment process of the analysand.

One challenge in the wealth management contract is that, just because you have no explicit mandate to make transference processes an explicit object of scrutiny does not mean they are not in the relationship. Arguably, the advisor discussed earlier was wading deep into a countertransferential quagmire where his reactions to what was occurring in the father-son dyad had everything to do with his own history with his father and blinded him to what was going on in the client system. This presents a particular challenge when there is a disconnect or deterioration in the client service relationship and there is no language for advisor and client to disentangle those things that may be part poor service, poor investment performance, and part transference from the client.

Yet this is not strange terrain for trust officers, for example, whose authority over assets often generates powerful feelings in both trustee and beneficiaries and can be difficult to parse out with respect to what issues are substantive and what related to the complex interpersonal relationship now set up by statute. In these cases, supported by an actual transfer of authority over assets in a quasi-parental and sometimes infantilizing manner, the emergence of a paternal transference to a trustee is far from unusual. This is why in many cases professional trust officers have come to talk about trusts as another sibling in the family or in other ways that personify the entity and the parties surrounding it. Unlike in the psychoanalytic situation, where the analyst can work a transference through so that the patient begins to dismantle a parental transference, a trustee-beneficiary dyad has the complication that the trustee really does have power over client assets. In the end, the wealth manager's challenge is that they have to manage these reactions both in their clients and in themselves where there is no presumption that analyzing transference is part of the wealth management value proposition. Because clients have been trained not to see you as a shrink does not mean that they will not bring to you material that should be dealt with using analytic or other psychological methodologies.

The wealth manager, by virtue of dealing with money in all its forms, zooms straight to the epicenter of significant transference reactions, if only because money and assets are at bottom symbolic instruments. *Money, in this sense, always means something else* and therefore invites any manner of lunacy to its environs. By implication, this means advisors will be reacting to reactions to them as advisors, and will witness—and react to—clients' reactions to the assets (mental accounting) and their containers, such as trusts, partnerships, and corporations. This is a formula for disaster for the advisor who knows little of how they themselves react to varying money conundrums and have not fine-tuned their own mechanisms for alerting themselves as to when they are reacting.

This becomes part of the rationale for *getting to know oneself with others*. Getting to know how you react to various assets and people and situations is not something to be done in isolation. You don't just go home and reflect by yourself on how you react to others and their assets and containers of assets. This kind of learning is a social process. We turn now to some of the ways self-knowledge can be expanded in advisors in ways that can have a practical bearing on how sophisticated your client intervention skills can get.

## Interpersonal Communications Training

The most basic level of awareness development comes through learning the basics of interpersonal communication. These kinds of training modules are widely available across a number of university-based environments and can help you dig into the basics of active listening, emotional labeling, and reframing. At this level, understanding how easy it is to be distracted from empathic engagement is often revealing, as is getting feedback on one's own interpersonal communication style.

Advanced methods, like those using Norman Kagan's Interpersonal Process Recall (IPR) methods take this a step further.[1] IPR has been used as basic training for therapists and counselors for decades. "The goals of IPR are to increase counselor awareness of covert thoughts and feelings of client and self, practice expressing covert thoughts and feelings in the here and now without negative consequences, and, consequently, to deepen the counselor/client relationship."[2] The basic framework uses video- or audiotaped segments between either a fellow class participant or a real client situation. With both individuals in the room, key tape segments are played and either person has the ability to stop the tape. Whoever stops the tape is asked to describe thoughts and feelings that were occurring at that time. Other participants in the training are encouraged to follow with nonjudgmental leads to aid in discovery of the range of thoughts, feelings, and perceptions occurring between the dyad. Some of these leads could include:

- What do you wish you had said to him/her?
- How do you think he/she would have reacted if you had said that?
- What would have been the risk in saying what you wanted to say?
- If you had the chance now, how might you tell him/her what you are thinking and feeling?
- Were there any other thoughts going through your mind?

- How did you want the other person to perceive you?
- Were those feelings located physically in some part of your body?
- Were you aware of any other feelings? Do they have any special meaning for you?
- What did you want him/her to tell you that they didn't?

Practicing this process over the course of a semester can palpably impact your awareness of how you react to people under various circumstances as well as how your reactions are perceived as on or wide of the mark. It is basic training in how to get out of your own way as regards interpersonal communications with high emotional content—for better or worse, the terrain in which the advisor increasingly finds him- or herself.

## Peer Supervision Groups

The other direction self-understanding can move through is a common practice used to train mental health practitioners in more advanced intervention techniques. Supervision in this context is where there is a regular meeting around which case presentations are made by one or more participants of clients they are working with. In some cases, these are run as peer supervision models where one receives questions and feedback on live cases that are presenting the advisor with some kind of challenge. Peers offer input and raise issues that may not be apparent to the case presenter. Often, the concentration is on the reactions of the presenter to various client issues that have emerged in the course of the work.

Supervision sessions for financial advisors—whether run by peers, a supervising expert, or guest experts—can provide a safe environment in which to dig deep into both psychodynamic and technical realms—that is, for financial advisors, they work at the level of both financial and interpersonal strategy. They can be run bimonthly or monthly either inside the firm or with outside participants. Organizers of these forums should pay attention to setting safe conditions for advisors to "let their hair down" with each other rather than heighten competitive aspects that drive the culture of these meetings toward black-and-white, right-and-wrong approaches dictated by an overbearing minority.

Supervision of this kind can really pick up speed for participants when a climate of trust sets the stage for analysis of transference and countertransference, as discussed above. The difference here is that you have now moved to a level where the reactions of supervision participants to each other and each other's cases begin to be used constructively to help unpack complex cases that may involve deploying complex financial strategies in dynamically charged families. This creates a high-intensity, high-value learning environment where insights about very practical matters remove blinders and psychological impediments for the advisor, rendering him or her more interpersonally agile in the room with dynamically complicated client scenarios. The supervisory forum also offers continuity of focus on cases: advisors can learn insights from their peers, generate hypotheses and courses of action to test, try it out, and come back to the supervision group to discuss how things went and what needs to happen next. This is not to mention the support and camaraderie that can unfold as advisors learn that they are not alone in this new land of intervening on families.

This kind of forum concretizes learning around the any number of areas to develop in advisors, including:

- The advisor's own history in relationship to money and family.
- Value frameworks advisors may be using more or less consciously with their clients.
- Blind spots advisors may have and ways to recognize them.
- Personal tendencies or styles of dealing with various situations.
- Approaches to conflict management, especially as regards money and wealth.

This model can also be a useful follow-up to classroom training as well. It enables you to keep insights fresh and to evolve a continuous cycle of learning that is specific to the new business you find yourself in.

## Tips and Takeaways for the New Financial Advisor

In the end, there are as many means and methods for getting to know yourself as there are people. The wide range of psychological and even spiritual approaches to this cannot be fully summarized in a book of this nature. The vehicles by which you do this will be up to you. How you take the journey may be less important than getting started. It is critical in doing this work to know yourself. It is nice enough to do this for yourself, but it is your clients who will also share in the benefit of having an advisor with "emotional intelligence" helping them navigate the sometimes rough waters of money and family life. To recap:

- If you don't find getting to know yourself important in its own right, do it for the sake of more finely tuning yourself as the most important instrument in the process of intervening on matters of wealth management. Do it, that is, for the sake of increased effectiveness in delivering integrated wealth management to complex financial families.

*(Continued)*

- Keep in mind that you are a *very* human agent in these matters and will have blind spots and various reactions to what you encounter. These are not problems as much as they are often sources of information that you can use to better understand what is going on in a client system.
- Any effort to deepen your understanding of yourself and how you work in complex client situations will be best done *with others*. Whether it is through formal training in interpersonal communications or through the establishment of peer supervision mechanisms, this learning process is a profoundly social endeavor and the strides you take are greatly enhanced when they are taken in concert with others who share in the goals of your journey.

# CHAPTER 4

# Service Model Supporting
# Life Outcomes

After reading the previous chapter, you might be worrying that once you change the way you work with clients you will fall down an interminable hole of family squabbles, and make massive, litigation-baiting missteps with your advice. If you wanted this type of interference, you say to yourself, you'd have become a shrink, a social worker, or a priest. The fact is, you are not in these other professions and you did not choose to be in them either.

Unlike a psychotherapist, your target of intervention is not to change the structure of personality; you are, however, in the business of facilitating effective psychological processes in your client systems because work with money and commoditized products puts you there. But what you do and what therapists do are very different endeavors. Working on character change makes character the object of long-term intervention strategies. This doesn't mean you won't create "therapeutic events" in what you do. The difference is that these events will not be by design but may occur as an artifact of major positive changes you initiate through a synthetic application of psychological and financial acumen. For example, I once worked with a family business that had an escalating conflict between the patriarch and his sons versus a couple of cousins in the business. Only one of these individuals would have ever remotely consented to therapy, but this was beside the point of the engagement. Teamed with an estate attorney, I intervened by walking the key stakeholder through a new shareholder and buy-sell funding arrangement that would diffuse mounting tension due to confusion between ownership and management succession for the business. The effects were dramatic, immediate, and, arguably, therapeutic. Focusing on character change, however, would have been a dead end. Using financial and legal information made all the difference in the lives of this family.

You are profoundly in the business of affecting life outcomes, and while the gravitas of your role should give you pause, a newly architected service model can help you manage any anxieties you may have.

This chapter presents a three-tier approach to service model development and helps the advisor think differently about the economics of the business as well. This three-tier model incorporates the following components into the totality of the service delivery system:

- A life-outcome orientation to your value proposition and business processes.
- Organization and infrastructure that supports your ability to deliver outcome-oriented services and do so with scale.
- A new economics that supports a life outcome–oriented business.

Everything from the value proposition to the technical infrastructure can be designed to support a life outcome–driven practice. This will be elaborated in this chapter, along with the implications for a range of practical issues, from contracting with clients to differences in the nature of each touch of the client system. Actual advisor-client dialogues will make these concepts real for the reader.

## Tier 1: Life Outcome Value Proposition and Supporting Processes

Providing great service begins with having a well-articulated value proposition. A value proposition is, in its simplest form, a set of promises about what you intend to deliver for a certain level of compensation. It also implies a particular scope of services that you are prepared to use to deliver against your promises. Advisors often bring unique propositions to bear on client issues and should not view what is said here to be restrictive. What is most important is alignment between the value proposition and services that support these propositions. Examples of alignment problems come into view in cases where, for example, the marketing function runs events that lead clients to believe that the firm has expertise in family dynamics or next generation financial learning and has little to support follow up needs clients express to their every day relationship manager. Promising the realization of life outcomes and delivering only investment returns is another example of disconnect between what is promised and what is actually delivered. To a large extent, this book is meant to help close that gap.

Once the value proposition and service mix is conceived, the questions of how services are delivered and how are they sustained emerge.

## Service Basics

At the most basic level, service models are often structured around something like the 12-4-1 model: Statements once a month, quarterly investment reviews, and an annual financial planning review. There are also touch points through other service channels, with significant efforts to architect Internet delivery to clients who prefer those forms of interaction. The basic service model represents what some have called a static model because it does not change much and serves to support "a core group of basic products and services—investment advisory, for example—that are widely expected."[1]

Variants from this model have to date been based on assets under management (AUM) models that have remained relatively constant. The CapGemini/Merrill Lynch World Wealth Report in 2007, in its spotlight on new service models, argues that "adopting a more dynamic service model puts clients on the receiving end of services that will satisfy their needs—and increase their lifetime value to the financial services provider—rather than those simply suggested by their AUM profile."[2] This dynamic model involves, among other thing, greater initial segmentation among clients for interests, cultural backgrounds, styles of interacting with the firm, communication preferences, and styles of behavior around financial matters. It also implies looking toward the potential lifetime value of a client system to the firm, rather than the immediate revenue streams represented by AUM metrics.

## Beyond the Basics

There is a presumption, then, that the basic service model is embedded in your firm—that the delivery of basic services relative to standard and compliant practices is in place. Your clients will get statements, have some form of Internet delivery of basic account information, and can call in to the firm's service center or service person when needed.

A service model oriented toward life outcomes has to first be able to discover what those outcomes are and develop a means to capture and monitor progress against them. To elaborate, we are talking about life outcomes as *demand-side outcomes* that require *supply-side components* that need to be *managed*. This means that they are outcomes as *articulated in the language of clients* rather than outcomes *defined by product or program results*.

Demand-side outcomes can, in my view, be best realized when clients are taken through the four core processes of wealth management. The names of these processes may change from firm to firm, but in their most basic form amount to the following:[3]

1. *Discovery.* This process involves examining a broad range of information about a client system and organizing this information into a set of problems that the sponsoring client is *willing to solve* with you.
2. *Solution Development.* In this process, the advisor takes the output of Discovery and turns back into the service and supply system—however limited or expansive this is—to assemble the team who will compose one or more solutions to be presented to the client system for feedback.
3. *Solution Deployment.* With an approved solution in hand, together with the system of meaningful metrics needed, the solution is launched and funded. This can mean a variety of moving parts are set in motion, from movement of money to setting up legal entities, inaugurating special projects, and initiating multiyear transfer strategies.
4. *Results Management.* This process commences upon funding and the completion of a results management protocol that enables each participant in the service delivery system to know exactly how to keep an eye on both macro and micro components of the solution, whether this is related to changes in asset valuations, asset mixes, interest rates, or entity compliance, or changes in the client system, such as the death of a principal or change in liquidity circumstances. As has been intimated above, this process is often the most important for the client and least supported by financial advisors and institutions. Doing this well opens multiple opportunities to go back into Discovery, as client system changes are picked up and responded to. Doing this poorly provides the mise-en-scène for a lost client, just when margins on this hard-won business widen.

The example of a couple who say that they would like to see their children be well educated can help unpack this concept. Several questions suggest themselves in Discovery mode:

- What does "well educated" mean to each member of the couple? College educated? Ivy-League educated? Includes graduate school? Does it mean business savvy? Street smart? Leadership and stewardship? Include financial literacy? How does the family history give shape to the concept? What role has formal education played for the family?
- On the human side, what is the current state of affairs for each of the children? All children good learners? Learning disabilities? Developmental disorders? Trouble in school for other reasons? In other words, what

are the existing assets and liabilities in human terms opposite these desired outcomes?
- On the financial side, what funding constructs are operative? Full funding for undergraduate and graduate education? Fund undergraduate only? Is the child asked to work and contribute, and if so, what shape should that take?

These questions start to help you build a demand-side outcome profile that is enriched by the detail behind the *management challenge* that is part of outcome realization. Recall that wealth *management* is being used broadly to convey all components of the management of wealth and factor them into how you evolve your proposition for the family. If every component behind educating the children falls into place—the family has a consistent history about education, the couple are on the same page about what education means and how it will get paid for, the kids are all perfectly capable learners and are on board with the funding concept—then you can turn seamlessly toward the supply-side components related to outcome realization. This means directing your attention toward traditional windows into whether there is adequate funding, whether that funding is as tax-advantaged as it should be, and whether there are potentially competing demands on funding resources. You can run economic models with or without children's contributions, Monte Carlo simulations, and gifting scenarios. You can develop investment policy statements that are nested in conventional risk tolerance constructs, as well as flag the possibility for alternative sources of funding based on possible catastrophic events. Because all of the human factors are in alignment, your proposition and service model require little extra effort. The client can be on-boarded in the customary way and the job will be priced accordingly.

If, however, every component behind educating the children does not fall into place—the couple is divided about what education means and how it should be funded, or the kids do not bring perfection to the learning process or even agree with the ends parents have in mind—you have another kind of wealth management challenge. The role of simply finding funding options will be insufficient to helping a client like this realize a life outcome. The very indication by the couple that all is not in perfect order will confront you with specific role choices you can take opposite the family, including:

- Ignoring what is being said.
- Being empathetic about what is being said but conveying that working on this is "not my job."
- Being prepared for unevenness and lack of perfection in the life outcome business and becoming part of the solution.

Your response to these three choices may be: What if one of the kids is learning disabled? Are you suggesting that I offer learning disability services as part of wealth management? Are you nuts? Or taking another possibility, that the couple is more than a little in disagreement with the educational issue. How should the advisor be positioned to help the couple, if at all?

Before examining service model options, the advisor should develop segmentation intelligence to help guide the evolution of the service architecture. Taking the above case, where a child is learning disabled, the advisor begins by asking, "How much of this kind of problem am I seeing?" If there is little of this in the families being seen, the service answer in the beginning is primarily related to the quality of referral sources you might have to private learning specialists, tutors, or other centers of expertise. There will be little value in wiring much more into your practice because you do not see the problem often enough to build out anything more than a stable of referral resources. On the other hand, if you are seeing this in some significant number of your client systems, you can take a number of business-building steps that begin to nest learning problems in a solution framework that might include some of the following:

- Host a seminar bringing in learning experts and invite existing and prospective clients.
- Develop a deeper bench of expertise in your referral resources that have distinct skill sets and let them know what steps you are taking to craft financial programs for this segment.
- Drive deeper into the financial conundrums that can attend comorbid syndromes with learning difficulties (e.g., children with learning problems sometimes have other problems, such as oppositional disorder, that can place kids in further educational jeopardy). Are there, for example, reward systems or best-practice allowance programs that build responsibility and heighten financial decision-making skills in this population? Are there special needs trusts or other trust strategies that support this kind of population and lend some comfort to parents with children with uncertain educational outcomes?
- Consider packaging services together into a component of your retainer fee such that attendance at seminars, learning assessments and financial literacy are bundled into a solution set for parents with children with learning challenges.

This kind of approach may or may not suit any number of advisors, not the least because they would not have the need or the resources to evolve such packaging. To reiterate: you are not a learning specialist and should not presume that I am pushing you this way. What you do bring to the table is a great deal of surrounding organizational and financial expertise that can connect the financial dots to a range of life outcomes that have a human and a financial component.

## Making Progress (While Making Money) Through Process Discipline

In the case where the couple is in substantial disagreement about the education agenda for the children, this can still take a different shape. Once again, the choice is always there to ignore intracouple dynamics, be empathic toward them but still do nothing, or evolve a service definition over time that points toward the life outcome of being better aligned as a couple around goal setting and financial decision making. Building a service model around achieving this outcome has much to argue for it. In a negative sense, you may have difficulty getting a couple to closure on any financial endeavor. Or you may find premature closure with one member of the couple only to experience substantial blowback from the other if they did not participate or felt slighted in the process. In a positive sense, making financial decision-making processes on the part of the couple a component of the service you deliver means you will get paid to help the couple move through this process rather than be at the mercy of whatever other decision-making drivers there are.

Recognizing this, The Legacy Companies train advisors in the use of, for example, questionnaires that allow couples to articulate their financial values separately and to see their similarities and differences reported back to them for resolution. They administer the Kolbe A test to assess decision-making styles for each. The couple is offered a chance to tell the story of their wealth—where it came from, what it should do, and where it should end up—as part of a developing attempt to synchronize their values with the way their underlying wealth is behaving with respect to these values.

This process is part of the Discovery process that clients go through and is usually paid for with a project-based fee. During the process, a wide range of data is collected, both financial and familial. Other resources, such as attorneys, accountants, and insurance professionals, are mapped, and a story begins to emerge around gaps in the wealth management team and in the alignment of client systems goals with the underlying structure and behavior of their wealth. If the conflict is high enough between the couple, consideration of a therapeutic team member may come up for the wealth manager. The issue is this: every client system that comes through your discovery process will present a current state of affairs and a long list of challenges to face down. Your job in Discovery is to narrow the list to those issues that the client is willing to allow you to help solve.

Once this list is determined, you move from Discovery to Solution Development. In the case of a couple in some distress around their ability to get on the same page about financial decision making, you have three principal options to consider in your Solution Development phase:

1. Bring a therapeutic expert onto the Solution Development team to help you strategize the work without getting directly involved (the individual supervision model).
2. Bring the case to a peer supervision format.
3. Contemplate an actual referral to possible therapists who may even coordinate their work with yours.

Keep in mind that the couple has proceeded through Discovery with you and is looking to you to help synchronize their family financial decision making. You may also determine that there is an educational component to the asynchrony apparent in the couple—that one member of the couple is comfortable with financial matters and the other virtually phobic, or that basic bookkeeping, budgeting, and bill-paying processes render one party in the know and another completely ignorant of what is going on.

Packaged together, you may develop a year-long retainer-priced program of customized family financial literacy utilizing your own resources and perhaps those of a financial psychologist (an emerging specialty) to deliver monthly sessions to the couple and quarterly meetings with other couples that are working on similar issues.[4] This may be step one of a multiyear process for proactively helping families proceed with decision making that does indeed gradually put them on the same page with one another. This is hardly therapy. It is not a treatment for an illness but a forward-leaning approach that will begin to differentiate your firm from others that claim to "help you reach your goals" but really only deliver supply-side solutions.

To move into the Solution Deployment phase, you need to make sure that you have some basics of scheduling and logistics and some project management capabilities. These are not complex services to deliver and they have the benefit of (1) being paid for, (2) managing the expectations about what you will be delivering, and (3) mitigating your fear that by engaging families around these kinds of issues you will find yourself running a clinic rather than an advisory firm. You need not fear boundary violations and abuse of your time. You can structure it to focus on positive movement and can bring in special expertise without the typically associated stigmas.

The Results Management phase enables you to monitor client progress throughout the life of the solution and offers a means by which changes to client systems or their underlying financial or business assets can surface and create the occasion to go back into Discovery and solve new sets of problems for clients. On the most basic level, you may be monitoring asset allocation tolerances and rebalancing issues, important tax changes or coming events, trust compliance, and philanthropic developments. At another level, you can informally survey your client families as to how they are doing and whether progress is being made with respect to financial literacy and decision-making processes between the couple. If your programs are not working, you will by now have credibility to ask if they wish to escalate their involvement or whether they want to work with a therapist, family business advisor, or the equivalent.

## Tier 2: The Organization and Infrastructure Supporting the Outcome-Oriented Business

Organization and infrastructure in this context refers to those socio-technical arrangements that enable the outcome-oriented business. It is not just technology. Instead, it reflects how you are organized, create a service culture, and implement the technology needed to both create efficiencies and scale and to differentiate your offerings.

It should be noted that the comments here are targeted primarily to small to medium-sized advisory firms and multifamily offices; and only to a lesser extent financial institutions, though the themes apply in general if not in detail.

To a significant extent, the thrust of this section draws from the crisis that a number of businesses have had to navigate in connection with a need to shift from product-centric to solution-centric organizations. These lessons learned have yet to be applied in financial service firms, in my view, because there has yet to be sufficient pain to enable this shift. Businesses like IBM, SunGard, and Nokia changed in ways that enabled them to stare down dire market circumstances and shift their organization and infrastructure to become profoundly more solution-oriented. IBM, for example, has moved from relying almost completely on product sales to deriving more than half of its annual revenue from its services and solutions. The financial advisory analogy can be found in moving away from AUM-dominated sources of revenue to revenue derived from outcome-oriented services.

### From Product-Centric to Client-Centric Services

Jay R. Galbraith has characterized the differences in product-centric versus client-centric businesses that are solution-oriented and these contrasts can be well-translated into the wealth management space.[5] As can be seen in Table 4.1, there is a palpable change in everything from goals and offerings to measures.

Galbraith's description of the product-centric business could not more profoundly describe the predominant form of financial advisory firm, as well as what might be written on the epitaph of many as the market moves away

TABLE 4.1  Organizational Changes for the Solution-Oriented Business (adapted from Galbraith, 2002)

| | Product-Centric Company | Client-Centric Company |
|---|---|---|
| Goal | **Best product for client** | **Best solution for client** |
| Value creation route | Cutting-edge products, useful features, new applications | Customizing for best total solution |
| Mental process | Divergent thinking: How many possible uses of this product? | Convergent thinking: What combination of products is best for this client? |
| Most important client | Most advanced client | Most profitable, loyal client |
| Priority-setting basis | Portfolio of products | Portfolio of clients—client profitability |
| Main offering | Specific products | Personalized packages of service, support, education, consulting |
| Organizational concept | Product profit centers, product reviews, product teams | Client segments, client teams, client P&Ls |
| Most important process | New product development | Client relationship management |
| Measures | • Number of new products<br>• Percentage of revenue from products < 2 years old<br>• Market share | • Client share of most valuable clients<br>• Client satisfaction<br>• Lifetime value of a client<br>• Client retention |
| Culture | New product culture: open to new ideas, experimentation | Relationship management culture: searching for more client needs to satisfy |
| Rewards | Based on business unit performance | Based on company performance |
| Approach to personnel | Power to people who develop products:<br>• Highest reward is working on next most challenging product<br>• Manage creative people through challenges with a deadline | Power to people with in-depth knowledge of client's business needs<br>• Highest rewardes to relationship managers who save the client's business |
| Sales bias | On the side of the seller in a transaction | On the side of the buyer in a transaction |

from the product-centric financial advisor. What this calls for is sustained attention to every aspect of your organization. These changes at the organizational level can be specifically identified for the financial service firm:

- *People.* You have to pay more than lip service to the notion that you need to get out of the weeds of administration and spend your time with clients and moving toward sitting on the same side of the table as them. Because you cannot will away your administrative and compliance functions, you have to source people to help you do this. At the same time, you also need to explore the use of junior analysts to do midrange financial project work, some of which must become billable. Your reward structures should tilt toward service milestones, such as those related to client retention. This is because nearly every important metric you have will relate to the problem that high-net-worth families are difficult to obtain and easy to lose—just when they become the most profitable. This also means that company profitability should drive incentives rather than revenue-centric rewards. You want to attract and retain profitable business in this new environment.
- *Process.* Most advisors optimize two types of processes: vertical and horizontal. Vertical processes are the ones you are most familiar with and relate to those surrounding your core product offerings. Your investment management process is an example, and many of you have squeezed efficiencies out of the process, but can probably do more, and ask for more from platform providers (see Chapter 7 for more on this theme). Horizontal processes are the processes typically neglected by advisory firms. Because this business has become multidisciplinary to the core, your integrating processes with other team members inside and outside your firm need more attention than ever. The more solution-centric you become, the more you will need integrating processes to nest component parts and service providers into well-orchestrated and personalized solutions. Rather than simply cross-referral relations, you will want to look at the ways in which the range of management and educational services can be more embedded in your offerings in more seamless ways.
- *Technology.* Most of what you view as mission-critical technology supports the vertical rather than the horizontal processes, and is therefore necessary but insufficient to deliver solutions. What you should be looking at are the following:
  - Customer relationship management (CRM) technology that is extensible into more horizontal applications.
  - Project extranet capability that enables you to rapidly assemble and disassemble teams inside and outside your firewall. This technology enables secure document sharing, and the basics of task and calendar

management to occur among estate planners, insurance professionals, and other resources that need to come together around specific client engagements.

- Professional services automation (PSA) products become important as your firm begins to look more like a consulting firm as you add, rationalize, and charge for more services.
- Applications to track time and billing. Because you will both be billing for more work and trying to understand relationship profitability, you will need more than month-end, back-of-the-napkin ways of understanding where people are spending time.
- Service-oriented architecture (SOA) platforms are a must for mid- to large-size advisory businesses. In a nutshell, these platforms enable technologies to talk and listen to one another without the expense of hard programming. These platforms are de rigueur for next generation Web-based service delivery.

- *Visibility.* Part of the new tilt in the technology agenda has a key client-side benefit, which is that you will begin to provide significantly greater visibility and transparency into what you do for clients. You need to bring important aspects of what you do out of the shadows so that you are in a great position to answer the question: "Why again am I paying you all these fees?" With the tools now available, documenting the *management side* of the wealth management business means that you enhance the visibility and value of the work you are doing for clients—and often can include them in Internet-delivered extranets that can create greater involvement in the value creation process as a whole.
- *Open product and service architecture.* In your new role as family-centric wealth manager, your value is driven by who you are and your ability to embed best-in-class product components and interdisciplinary expertise in personalized solutions. In many but not all cases, this means you have to open your organization to other providers and develop your value as the talent manager and orchestrator of solution components. Your role as choreographer becomes a value driver with revenue implications.

## Tier 3: Toward a New Economics of the Advice-Based Business

In this section, I first want to address what for many of you will be a looming question about the implications in this model for recurring revenue. After reading about the first two tiers of the service development model, you may be thinking that the emphasis on moving away from product and underwriting fees toward project and retainer relationships renders your revenue characteristics less attractive. In the first instance, I like recurring revenue as much as the next person, but here are some comments to think about as you ponder your new client-centric approach:

- Depressed valuations and the resulting poor exit strategies for owners should be a message that in many cases the market views these businesses more like consulting firms. Recurring revenue is tied so intimately to the "producer" that the market does not share your internal view of the quality of the revenue.

- Selling a product to a family and expecting them to stick around assumes that product is going to be different enough and valued enough to keep their interest over time. Experience shows, however, that families are difficult to obtain and easy to lose, just at the time the real profitability begins to be realized. This is partly a function of a negative response to "what have you done for me lately?"

- Product sales alone push you toward being a bit-player in the family's life, whereas ongoing projects with clients more deeply make you aware of what is going on in the family and further instantiate you as the go-to firm for services.

- Projects and retainer jobs have tiered pricing and involvement from your staff and, as a result, encourage a relationship with your firm and not just with the individual advisor. Strong companies develop working alliances with families as a firm, even though it is the quality of the people that count in the end.

- Handled appropriately, these other kinds of engagements not only generate opportunities to bring products into the family but enable you to more continuously monitor how well they are embedded in and functioning on behalf of life outcomes.

So make no mistake. What is proposed here is designed to shift your business economics toward making your revenue more durable—and diversifying it at the same time.

## Changing the Revenue Mix

A reorganized business and infrastructure does little if in the end the business is not profitable and has not increased its annuity value. In this section, the case is made for changing the framework for the economic model underlying the outcome- or solution-oriented business. Because of the nature of the change proposed, you should not attempt to do this over night. If need be, make the changes in small increments. If you do begin this now, by the time this new wave is coming, it will be "surf's up" for your business. Figure 4.1 illustrates how your revenue streams can change over time to reflect your increasing penetration into the family outcome advisory business.

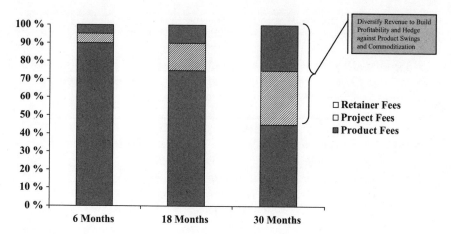

FIGURE 4.1  Planned Change in Revenue Mix for the Outcome-Oriented Advisory Business

Philosophically, what you are trying to do from an economic standpoint is start to look at client profitability and lifetime value to the firm. Having *client profitability* as the key driver also begins to shift your whole business in relationship to clients and provides a metric for assessing your progress. *Lifetime value* similarly reinforces a view into client systems that may include but is less dominated by transactions. Conceiving of your own human resources in light of their possible *billability* in client engagements can also contribute toward a positive transformation in the economics of your business.

> *Client profitability.* There are times in the life of a business when revenue generation should be top of the agenda. However, for most readers of this book, the profitability of clients should and can ascend to the top. For most, this will mean segmenting your book of business into service levels over some period of time and will reorient you toward the kind of business you will be transitioning to in the future. Using three service levels usually helps begin this transition, with Level 3 clients being product-centric clients, where you are getting underwriting, product, or asset management fees. Level 2 clients are hybrid clients, where there is an opportunity to mix some amount of project or retainer fee in with product fees. Level 1 clients are advisory clients, where there is substantial opportunity for larger project or retainer fees and where their use of your product suite may be possible but unclear until later in the work. The key to profitability is to match resources with jobs using a tiered approach that you can customize for your firm.

*Lifetime value of clients.* When screening prospects and generating initial engagements, your orientation should shift from questions like "What is the AUM opportunity?" or "What is the commission opportunity?" to "What does the multiyear, intergenerational scenario look like for this family and how can I provide services along the way?" This means that instead of turning away from, for example, a family business client because of the dominance of illiquid assets in the total picture, you reorient yourself toward what services you might provide over a period of years that would add value to the many family and familial decisions that will need to be made as the family and business cycle through their various developmental phases. Many wealth managers leave behind the real annuity potential of their business by basically ignoring the children and grandchildren of the couples they serve. What solutions can you provide in your new role as an "objective" advisor that stand to support your penetration of the extended family as a trusted advisor? Assistance with family governance issues? With liabilities and risks management? Coordinating financial management services? Help with capital and shareholder liquidity dynamics? In your new role as an advisor who is not simply hooked to a product sale, you have a range of intervention opportunities that will enable you to be the go-to firm for families for many years and into the next generations—all at a substantially reduced cost of sale.

*Billability.* Another consideration is to reexamine your staffing plan through the lens of billability. Transforming your staff from pure overhead to billable assets can take time but should run concurrently with other changes you are making to reorient your business away from old business models. You are already preparing to segment your clients into different groups against which you will apply differing service models over time. You can also do this with the work itself; that is, segment it, place a value on it, and staff it accordingly. When I run complex projects with clients, I use a simple tool like the one illustrated in Figure 4.2 to help segment the work and price it competitively and defensibly.

## What Can I Charge For?

There is a range of wealth management services that clients may need to procure over their life span. Table 4.2 illustrates a few core wealth services and those that involve management services.

Table 4.2 is not meant to provide an exhaustive outline of the kinds of services for which you can charge fees, but to be suggestive of the range of engagements that are being paid for by clients, in many cases through project or retainer-like arrangements.

| Item | | Partner | Sr. Analyst | Jr. Analyst | Admin. | Outside Expert | Outside Expert | Outside Expert | Total |
|---|---|---|---|---|---|---|---|---|---|
| **Resource** | | | | | | | | | |
| **Daily Rate Schedule** | | $3,200 | $1,600 | $1,000 | $750 | $1,600 | $1,200 | $1,200 | |
| **Effective Hourly Rate** | | $400 | $200 | $125 | $94 | $200 | $150 | $150 | **Total** |
| **Jones Discovery Project** | | | | | | | | | |
| Kickoff preparation | | 0.25 | 0.25 | | 0.25 | | | | $1,388 |
| Kickoff meeting | | 0.50 | 0.50 | | | | | | $2,400 |
| Primary discovery | | 0.25 | 0.75 | 0.75 | | | | | $2,750 |
| Secondary discovery | | 0.25 | 0.50 | 0.75 | 0.50 | 0.50 | | | $3,525 |
| Compilation/initial analysis | | 0.25 | 0.50 | 0.50 | | | | | $2,100 |
| Review of initial findings with client | | 0.25 | 0.25 | | | | | | $1,200 |
| Revisions | | 0.25 | 0.25 | | 0.25 | | | | $588 |
| Final deliverable presentations | | 0.25 | 0.25 | | | 0.25 | | | $1,600 |
| | | | | | | | | | $0 |
| | | | | | | | | | $0 |
| | | 2.00 | 3.25 | 2.00 | 1.00 | 0.75 | 0.00 | 0.00 | **$15,550** Total Fees |
| | | | | | | | | | **7.000** Total Days |
| | | | | **Estimated Days** | | | | | |

**$278** Blended Rate/Hr.

FIGURE 4.2 Project Pricing Sheet (For Internal Use)

TABLE 4.2    Wealth Management Services

| Core Wealth Services | Management Services |
| --- | --- |
| Strategic Wealth Design | Discovery Services |
| Estate Planning | Wealth Team Management |
| Income Tax Planning | Information Management (Online Archive) |
| Risk and Insurance Planning | Cash Management & Budgeting |
| Business Succession Planning | Family Mission Statement Development |
| Investment Management | Special Project Management |
| Asset Protection Planning | Family Constitution & Governance |
| Retirement Planning | Financial Literacy Programs |
| Philanthropic Planning | Customized Wealth Coaching |
| Asset Monetization | Family Meeting Services |
| Banking and Credit | Family Office Services |

One example of how to structure financial arrangements with clients might work is to unhook Discovery and Solution Development processes from the underwriting or investment management sale. This means that you sell these services stand alone for project-based fees rather than doing the up-front work for free. Doing so achieves three things right away:

1. You are getting paid to identify the wealth management problem set and to help your client system sort and evaluate the elements of that set, while choosing which of these components they want you to help them with.
2. You are declaring that there is not automatic sale of a product on the back end and that the solutions you architect with the client will be profoundly about them.
3. You are setting an expectation that the fuller range of services you deliver are valuable in their own right and are not simply more sophisticated traps set for another end game, such as a product sale.

In other words, you are repositioning your value proposition away from product salesperson to solution generator. Depending on the estimated net worth and complexity of the client system, these jobs can be priced in the $5,000 to $50,000 range. Your proposal can build in a discount on subsequent services should the client decide to do further work with you through follow-on services that may still not be related to product sales but rather, for example, ongoing wealth strategy development and team management, bundled with an extranet web site where the client can monitor project developments.

Advisors often have issues with new pricing concepts, to some extent because of issues with money generally—as we have argued in Chapter 3, advisors are hardly free of these concerns. Keith Whitaker at Wachovia says that we should:

> *Add to this how the issue of pricing has been complicated because we have taught clients for decades that if they just give us the money to manage, everything else will come for free. We have been enablers of this tendency and are having to work through the consequences.*[6]

Other leaders in the field have consistently argued that families themselves need to be educated about pricing and subsequently about the value of the strategies you are implementing for them over a period of time.

There are also embedded issues and debates related to active versus passive management and how these processes play out for individual firms in the current climate. The short answer—admittedly easier said than done—is to begin charging for value created. Experiments down this path suggest that where there is perceived value, people will pay for the service. Charging only AUM fees and keeping your integrating and management work in the shadows may work in the short run in bullish markets, but charging for time and services—periodic and recurring—which are visible to clients and help them realize life outcomes will help you smooth out your revenue streams and materially affect client profitability.

---

## Tips and Takeaways for the New Financial Advisor

Changing your service model is a big job and should be implemented in stages. There are key assumptions you can use along the way to screen the different steps you consider taking and to help you develop timelines and priorities. These include:

- *Time.* Your and your client's time is extremely valuable and is to be used wisely. Every element of the service model should be screened for its impact on time.
- *Profitability.* Model elements should be vetted for their contribution to profitability in either positive or negative ways. Though often easier said than done, this screen should be rigorously applied to all service components—something that is often new to advisors and not easy to apply.
- *Cross-subsidization* of services should be minimized. The model where assets under management, for example, should be the revenue stream by which everything else gets funded should be challenged at every step.

- *Payment for Services.* Related to the point above, of course, is that services for "free" should be phased out. Anything that consumes the time of you or your staff that is not normal overhead, genuine marketing expenses and the like should be evaluated as a component of pricing or phased out.
- *Reeducating clients and referrals.* Clients and referral sources will need to be educated on what you are doing. As you change, you should not be surprised if others around you do not suddenly get it and release you easily from the box into which you have placed by industry history and your own participation in it.
- *Selectivity.* Because you are now more in a business characterized by client intimacy does not mean you will accept all clients, including those that are perpetually difficult or abusive. Good practice management, even in the therapeutic world does not allow for abuse, nor does it imply the absence of rules and boundaries. Good service practices will help you select, mitigate and manage highly charged situations. Risk management principles derived from mental health professions can actually provide elements of a framework through which to evaluate the risk parameters of your engagements.
- *Supply-side technology.* Supply-side technology investments—portfolio management systems, financial planning engines, underwriting tools, trading systems—should be reviewed for their necessity as part of your value proposition and, if possible, examined for outsourcing potential, as should standard desktop applications that can be distributed via managed desktops. This means that, where possible, you should get out of the technology and hosting businesses. This will not apply, of course, to institutional sponsors where there may be solid business reasons to take a proprietary approach to technology.
- *Demand-side technology.* Demand-side technology investments—professional service automation, work flow, project management, notification engines—should command your attention because they will more directly support your actual work. Further, they should be consumed as services where possible (through application service providers, or ASPs) as well. There is increasingly little need for you to run proprietary applications on your desktops and servers. This is not a core competency and brings increasing risk and expense to the equation.

From here, we turn toward family meetings as a key component of service delivery that warrants close attention for the new financial advisor.

# CHAPTER 5

# Facilitating Family Meetings

Family meetings are both overhyped and underdeveloped as a tool for financial advisors. They have become front-and-center offerings in wealth businesses from Citibank to Wachovia, but a real source of anxiety to advisors on the vanguard of dealing with complex financial families. On the one hand, the literature on family meetings is compelling with respect to family and family business outcome variables. Frequency of family meetings is a leading predictor of, for example, the likelihood that a family intending to pass a family business from one generation to the next will actually succeed in doing so.[1] As a result, you are once again presented with an opportunity to augment your practice in a way that will challenge you to develop new skills. In this chapter, you will learn about different types of family meetings and when to use them, and the ABCs of how to prepare, execute, and follow through. This chapter is about demystifying family meetings and helping you carry them off with increased confidence. It will outline what is meant by family meetings and develop a typology of meetings so advisors know how to better plan and execute these meetings. We also review family meeting best practices, basic facilitation techniques, and, last but not least, your "worst fears" about running family meetings and ways to manage through difficult meeting situations.

## What Are Family Meetings?

Financial advisors use a variety of face-to-face encounters with clients to move various service processes along. Meeting with couples to discuss issues of planning or execution is commonly part of financial service delivery systems, particularly where spousal buy-in will be needed down the road for implementation of strategies or products. Family meetings are a variant of this mechanism that can strongly affect the kinds of outcomes clients are seeking. Professional facilitators have stepped in to do this work at the high end of the market, but even in these segments, use of professional facilitators is not always practical, nor is it even necessarily desirable. Financial advisors have tremendous advantages when they can do this work themselves, but it has to be done in concert with changes we have discussed about value propositions and service processes. It is not enough to suddenly offer "family meetings" as a new service if nothing else in how you approach clients has changed.

Family meetings, conventionally understood, should be used in the most basic situation where there is a need to bring the actual systemic representatives of the voices in a client's context *into the room in order to hear them speak for themselves*. The clarity that can be derived about the dynamic force field in which decisions are being made that can be obtained when the other players bring their perspectives should not be underestimated. What might have seemed in individual meetings to be a resistance to taking a certain action now becomes comprehensible as a genuine concern that a key stakeholder might have surrounding the decision. You can see and hear the pushback in living color and surround sound. You'll now understand what may have been previously inscrutable reluctance or resistance on the part of your client.

As with many things related to "family," things are not always what they seem when it comes to family meetings. In the first instance, there are two obvious types of family meetings that we might be referring to in a financial advisory process. The first is FAMILY MEETINGS, the capital letters version that has been promoted throughout the industry in recent years. These meetings are highly choreographed encounters, often taking place in neutral locations, such as a hotels or resorts, and usually have significant financial and emotional relevance to the various family members. Examples of these can occur around senior-generation disclosure of estate planning strategies to the family, developing a system for family governance, discussing major family business decisions, or working on a shared philanthropic vision and strategy. These more structured meetings can provide a meaningful and useful answer to overly tactical, divisive, or ineffectual communications among members. They invite a seriousness of purpose and a sense that being a family in a larger sense actually matters and warrants a new level of seriousness in interactions.

The second global type of family meeting is one that is substantially less formal. In some ways, family meetings are always going on, usually in fragmentary encounters and along lines of existing familial alliances. For example, two members who work in the family businesses may meet frequently and, for better or worse, leave out other family members who may also be business owners but do not work in the business day to day. Equally, some family members may be on the phone multiple times a day with each other—again, usually along alliance lines that may have become entrenched over years or decades.

This means that, in an important sense, the kinds of meetings orchestrated by financial advisors are in many ways *interruptions* in the typical flow of meetings and communication among families. Because they deal with money and because money is deeply private and interwoven with other family dynamics, these interruptions are also interventions in the most basic sense: your work will change the normal flow of family discourse. It can do this in a way that is either trivial, ineffectual, and undermining or meaningful and progressive.

To complicate this further, in reality family meetings are going on even when you think they aren't. This is critical. The issue is this: even when you are talking to only one visible member of a family, you are still talking to a group. This may seem counterintuitive, but the laws of language and the formation of personality offer a powerful argument that none of us is ever completely alone. This operates on at least two levels—the individual level and the family level.

On the individual level, we are a concatenation of voices and narratives about who we are that we have been actively rehearsing and reinventing our whole lives. A simple and obvious example of this might be when you catch yourself "sounding like your father" as you discipline one of your teenage children. Similarly, the structure of guilt and conscience are highly derivative of the internalization and personalization of social laws and personal upbringing. They operate as incorporated scripts that drive what we do and connect to broader narratives that both define us and make the redefinition of ourselves a creative possibility. These processes are not typically conscious processes any more than you contemplate individual words you string together to form a spoken sentence or pump the brake when approaching a red traffic light. The fact that these voices emanate from an individual speaker does not nullify their profoundly social origins. And conversations about money are no less social and familial in origin.

On a family level, speaking to a married individual as if the spouse is not also "in the room" in some fashion is naive and shortsighted. The work of "individual" psychotherapy demonstrates this time and again. Clients bring their whole families and more into the consulting room, whether physically or not. Trying, for example, to keep an alcoholic sober using individual therapy alone is by now completely known to be a broken play. To imagine this is somehow not the case in client interactions in a financial service context is to risk naiveté at the least or, worse, to generate or collude with destructive processes nascent or evolving in the family. Estate planners know that a process of unilateral conversations with one member of a family system often leads to a failure to execute the estate strategy because of unexplored blowback or ambivalence that attends big decisions that have important and often irrevocable consequences.

One estate planner I know learned of the need to actively incorporate both spouses' interests the hard way. He had worked with a couple for several meetings, when it was decided that the wife did not need to be in all of the meetings where, among other things, they were contemplating execution of a complex strategy resulting in substantial generation-skipping trusts being set up for young grandchildren. Her comment that she did not need to be in "all these technical discussions" was accepted at face value. Apparently harmless to begin with, this inadvertently exclusionary process led the attorney in retrospect to believe that he did not sufficiently pick up "Mom's" cues around her ambivalence about the consequence of creating grandchildren who would be substantially wealthier than her children. Maybe Mom didn't need all the detail, but the gist of where things were headed was far from lost on her. Meanwhile, Dad had become enamored of, if not virtually obsessed with, the tax efficiencies of the plan and the growth projections of the financial wealth itself. Mother's quiet withdrawal was not an assenting vote to the process, but a passive protest against the estate planning train that seemed to have left the station. As in other decision patterns the couple had developed over many years of marriage, the wife knew she did not need to participate in the celebration of the technical genius of the strategy in order to pull out the veto pen later.

The attorney never saw Mom again. In fact, after a comprehensive drafting of the estate strategy, all that was left was to execute the documents and begin funding processes. Attempts to schedule this seemingly pure transactional event were first casually pushed out a couple of weeks. Then came the first cancellation, and the second. The attorney finally got Dad on the phone only to find that the couple was going to hold off on signing the document because they were just too busy. When pressed, the father conceded that the mother had "leaked" the evolving estate strategy to two of the oldest kids, who in turn ambushed Dad with their own "family meeting" around what could he possibly be thinking by unilaterally driving the financial future of their families in this way.

This example, for current purposes, does not suggest that Mom and/or the kids should have been part of every meeting. It does argue for earlier use of a family meeting format as part of the Discovery and Solution Development processes. But even when this is not practical, what it really suggests is that even in conversations with Dad, the idea that multiple forces and voices would play on him through any process having these stakes should tilt even individual discussions toward exploration of the family embeddedness of this decision. It is so easy to fall in love with a strategy, especially when you have a willing audience in the family member who is writing your check, yet the love can blind you to all-too-important contextual components of the individual psyche.

# Typology of Family Meetings

This leads us to sharpen the question as to what type of meeting should be contemplated in different situations. The most basic way experts have typed meetings of any kind is to organize them along the lines of the purpose of the meeting being planned along two axes—content intensive and process intensive.

Content-focused meetings refer to technical matters and financial details. The need to convey a complex investment concept, to provide an analysis of the family's balance sheet, or to evaluate tax implications of different approaches to selling one's company are instances of a more highly content-driven purpose. Process-focused meetings concentrate less on what is being discussed (financial content in most cases) and more on how decisions are being made. Process-centric meetings draw attention to the relationship side of things. How democratic are things going to be? How will we weigh privacy versus openness? How unilaterally or multilaterally will we treat family financial matters? In other words, whether a 60/40 equities-to-fixed income portfolio is better in the client's case than a 50/50 portfolio is of less interest than *how* the couple is making the decision and *what* the decision tells of their different beliefs in regard to what these portfolios mean.

To make a more stark contrast: a content-centric meeting might be an attorney describing the ownership succession plan to a family group whereas a process-centric meeting might focus on how the client family wants to develop the succession plan in the first place. Content meetings convey data and information. Process meetings concentrate on how learning and decision making occurs or should occur. Content says: here are some fish; process says: shall we go fishing, how have you fished in the past, and can we help you learn to fish better as time goes on?

These two broad meeting types are not meant to reflect pure states or differences of purpose in meetings. That is, there is no meeting that does not have content and process. They are inseparable. You can no more run a pure process meeting than speak a sentence without words, as if how you say something could be completely divorced from what you said. More importantly, the reason for this distinction is to identify what kind of meeting is being staged and, in particular, what the facilitator is going to concentrate on and the direction his or her interventions are going to take. This means that the things I pay attention to and ignore as a facilitator are going to change depending on the type of meeting being run. The core focus of the meeting will drive those things that will be tabled or placed in the "parking lot" for later attention. Thus, if I am simply delivering quarterly investment results, I am going to pay attention to different kinds of meeting dynamics than if I am working with a family on the design of a family mission statement or a family trying to liquefy a dissident sibling shareholder in the family business. Figure 5.1 illustrates these differences and provides some examples of meeting types.

## Synchronizing Purpose with Design

The type of meeting you wish to facilitate should be driven by the type of intervention you are trying to orchestrate. In turn, the type of meeting should drive the design of the meeting, as is illustrated in Figure 5.2.

Your lead-up to a meeting requires you to focus on your process for doing this as well. For example, how will you decide the purpose of the meeting? Unilaterally or with help from members of the client system? Which members of the client system will you engage for this purpose? If your approach to meeting design is open, how will you respond to a client system whose historic tendency is to make decisions in a unilateral and closed manner? Will the very act of generating the purpose of a meeting itself need to be viewed as an intervention? How hard should you push for early inclusiveness? How will you know when you've pushed too hard? These questions don't lend themselves to cookbook answers but do tie

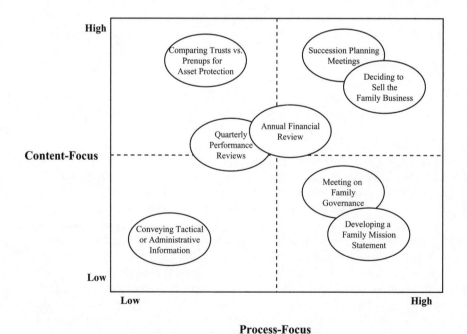

FIGURE 5.1 Sample Meeting Types Based on Weighting of Process- and Content-Centric Purposes

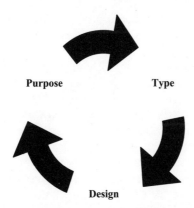

**Purpose**          **Type**

**Design**

FIGURE 5.2  Synchronizing Family Meeting Purpose, Type, and Design

into your understanding of your own style, values, and approach to service processes.

**CONTENT-CENTRIC DESIGNS**    Paying attention to the purpose of the meeting itself puts you in a good position to design the meeting. If the meeting's purpose is primarily to deliver content, your attention should turn to how this content should be presented. Content-centric meetings imply that you, as the advisor, and your team know something that is not well known or known at all to your client. This does not imply that what you do will be dry and dull, but does suggest that you pay attention to some of the following issues as you prepare for the meeting:

- Is what is presented something that the audience will already know how to assimilate, or does there need to be an educative process? If your audience knows well the difference between a stock and a bond, is familiar with asset allocation and related risk and return concepts, understands performance indices, and you are delivering quarterly performance results, you probably would not classify this as an educational meeting and would mostly require simple reporting.
- What about the media itself? I once held a family meeting with a billionaire who could take one look at a complex, unlabeled spreadsheet and correct the errors on it, and his daughter, for whom we had to color-code buckets of money according to red (don't touch this), yellow (don't touch this unless you have to), and green (use this money prudently but how you see fit). Same family. Bright people. Different information consumption styles.[2]

- Does the meeting have an educational component? If there is an educational agenda, several issues should be considered that will affect the effectiveness of your approach:
  - What are the learning styles of your target audience? The notion of "differentiated instruction" is highly applicable here. Differentiated instruction takes into account the reality that individuals each learn differently and that instruction should vary along the lines of (1) *content* (multiple options for taking in information), (2) *process* (multiple options for making sense of the ideas), and (3) *product* (multiple options for expressing what they know).
  - Is there a larger educational agenda being pursued? Differentiated instruction allows for further consideration around alternatives for expanding *depth, complexity, novelty,* and *pacing.* This may mean situating the meeting itself in a larger pedagogical framework that empowers rather than disables learners with different styles.

Notice that even if the meeting is content-centric, there is no reason to imagine that process considerations aren't operative. Again, we are really talking shades of emphasis and what you, as a facilitator, focus on. Content meetings can be orchestrated to become highly interactive, depending on the learning style of the constituents.

**PROCESS-CENTRIC DESIGNS**   Perhaps the more anxious terrain for many advisors is the meeting that is more explicitly process-centric. These may be meetings in which the sources of the knowledge are in some way reversed from what they are in content meetings: the knowledge is resident in, for example, the family system and needs to be teased out. Process-centric meetings have as their purpose an intervention that seeks to change how a family does things. Examples of meetings that tilt toward process-related purposes might include the following:

- Meetings to improve family financial decision making.
- Meetings to introduce conversations that have heretofore either not taken place or have proceeded only with much difficulty.
- Meetings on matters of family governance.
- Meetings to kick off family projects.
- Meetings to design a family mission statement or family financial philosophy.
- Meetings to generate key decisions around a family foundation, such as charter building or determination of causes and strategies.
- Meetings to decide who should come to which meetings (as in, for example, the case of in-laws at a family council retreat or nonfamily executives at family business board meetings).

These are meeting types that usually require more attention to design components—the architecture and timing of meeting activities, and the roles participants will play—and facilitation strategies. A "facilitator" role is often invoked in these contexts to convey that the individual convening the meeting and setting out the rules is doing so knowing that the family needs to begin to construct and arrive at its own truths. More so than in content-centric meetings, the position of "expert" is ceded to the position of "facilitator" by the advisor in recognition that the family itself uses its own authority and creativity to evolve itself. The work of the facilitator is to set the conditions under which this can take place in the most optimal way.

The design and facilitation components of putting these meetings often challenge advisors to upgrade these skills—something we will revisit in Chapter 8. Inexperience here often leads advisors to over- or underengineer these experiences, leaving significant promise of a highly meaningful service encounter lying fallow in chaos or its opposite. Depending on the stakes and focus of the meeting, the advisor may do well to consider partnering with a professional facilitator who knows the wealth management space—which is also an important way to upgrade your skills.

## Summary of Best Practices

Running an excellent family meeting is very much like painting: much of it is in the preparation. At the same time, meeting execution and post-meeting follow-through are dimensions of the family meeting intervention as a whole that are most visible and memorable to the participants. Paying attention to the items below will give you a way to make sure you have done what it takes to set the stage for a quality experience, keeping in mind that a quality experience does not uniformly mean a cheery experience for every participant. In fact, quality progress against any intervention strategy usually does not come without some amount of pain. Once you have decided the purpose of the meeting and what kind of meeting you are trying to execute, these steps will help you anticipate and optimize your meetings:

### Before
- *Visualize the experience.* Who is in the room? Where are you? What kind of activity is going on? What surroundings will support your purposes? What role are you playing? Are you in the foreground? Background? Facilitator? Or content provider?
- *Establish objectives and an agenda.* Are your objectives SMART objectives as much as possible (Specific, Measurable, Achievable, Realistic, and Timed)? Does the family have a real chance to make headway?

Does the agenda tie to the objectives and identify who will be doing what in support of these objectives?

- *Determine attendance.* Is there clarity about who is coming? Do you know the players, including any third-party players? Do you know their personal profiles and agendas—overt or covert—for the meeting?
- *Select the venue and anticipate logistical issues.* Is the choice of venue and the logistics around it conducive to the realization of objectives or in the way? For example, don't put families in auditorium seating if you are facilitating a meeting on family governance, or don't generate tasks that require writing while having a meal arrive.
- *Prepare participants.* What should participants have done before they arrive? Is there material that should be consumed privately before the meeting (a draft of a document, background information on the topic, an article or two on the themes of the meeting)? Have you talked to meeting participants and vetted the agenda in person or at least by telephone?

## During
- *Set the stage and tone.* Do you have an introduction that fits with the tone you want to set? Do you need an icebreaker of some kind?
- *Review the agenda and objectives.* You may have done this in the ramp-up to the meeting, but it can be important for participants to see and feel each other assent to the objectives and agenda.
- *Establish ground rules.* Do any ground rules need to be set? These can provide teaching moments around process matters that are useful to family members who are unfamiliar with what it means to pay attention to process (versus content). This also shows that the facilitator is in charge of the "container" in which the meeting will unfold (the room, keeping time, preventing intrusions or distractions), but that the participants will largely police themselves within a set of rules. Sample ground rules might include variants of the following:
  - All ideas are valid.
  - Participate fully.
  - Take risks.
  - Convey respect.
  - Have your say, and listen to others.
  - All participants are equal.
  - No mobile phones.
  - One meeting at a time.
  - Be punctual.
- *Manage the agenda.* Are you in control of the agenda? Are you prepared to make judgments about deviating from the agenda and to share the basis of these judgments with participants? Do you have space for "parking lot" items, that is, those items that come up and should be

archived and addressed later but do not currently serve to advance the obtainment of objectives?

■ *Focus your attention on what is really going on.* Are you paying attention to the content, delivery, and affect of each of the parties? What is it telling you? What conflicts are brewing or being buried? Are they conflicts that relate to objective attainment or are they distractions that you should park? Is there an "elephant in the living room"? Do your questions sound like they are being delivered by an expert or a fellow explorer? Where is there common ground? Where are important differences? Are rules being broken, and if so, what significance do you apply to it? What kinds of resistance are emerging in whom?

■ *Archiving the meeting.* Is it appropriate for someone to take notes? Will the family be generating material for flip charts? Is there a way to capture or photograph the white or blackboard being used?

■ *Finishing the meeting.* Have you taken sufficient time to summarize and conclude the meeting? Have next steps been identified and any assignments made? Have you made time to allow participants to evaluate what has happened and to offer constructive feedback?

**After**

■ *Debriefing.* Have you gone back to family leaders and asked what they made of the meeting? Other participants?

■ *Following through.* Have you the means to check in with and track progress? What kinds of barriers have emerged? What steps can be taken to support follow-on work?

■ *Evaluating your effectiveness.* Have you taken the time to review how you did and what you might want to do better? What feedback can you glean from co-facilitators or other experts in support of how you did? Have you asked them in advance to keep an eye on how you do certain things and followed up on their observations?

# Facilitation Basics

Most meeting types require some form of facilitation skill. These skills will be touched on later in Chapter 8, but there are some basic rules presented here that should serve to keep you on track in most types of basic meetings where you have a reasonably well-functioning family or group.

■ *Strive for inclusiveness and constructive member participation.* Pay attention to the form of participation members are presenting, and how the group is managing speaking and silence. One does not have to be speaking to be actively participating, but an excess of silent participation is generally something to move against in these meetings.

- *Don't panic when it seems that too much is going on.* Many novice facilitators struggle with the sheer volume of information flowing in a meeting. So do advanced facilitators, with the difference being the comfort taken in the concept that if something is important enough and you miss it the first time around, it will come up again. When facing potentially complex facilitations, even the best facilitators will not do it alone and have a partner in the room to increase the probability that things won't be missed and that working hypotheses about what is going on can be validated with another expert.
- *Track who is saying what to whom.* Family meetings, like other human encounters, are like stagings of nonfiction drama where part of what you are listening for are roles and voice. Tracking who is speaking to whom and in what role can be extremely helpful in guiding what you pay attention to. Sometimes, asking a speaker to identify who they are and who they are talking to can be extremely clarifying. For example, if a father barks at his daughter in a meeting on family business matters, you can ask if he is responding to her as her boss or as her father, and check with the daughter to see if she is hearing him as her father or boss. Equally, speakers of overly general statements to the group as a whole can be invited to better specify their audience. Often, you will know this is happening when someone is using "we" excessively or presumptively, as in "we think there is an insufficient allocation to non-U.S. securities" when, in fact, they are speaking only for themselves. Because the management of wealth often requires the same person to assume many roles, it is often very useful to sharpen the group's perception of how these voices move in and out and either clarify or obscure what's going on. As in the case of the presumptive *we,* the facilitator can both urge the person to use an "I-statement" and then inquire as to whether others agree or disagree.
- *Follow the language and the story.* To carry further the notion of meetings as drama, one can also track the storyline and the language individuals are using to articulate their characters. Paying attention to metaphors can, for example, provide the family with feedback and new insight into how they are orienting themselves to the issues at hand.
- *Stay orthogonal to the players and issues.* In most cases, you will want to avoid taking sides of individuals or issues that really require work and focus on the part of the family. An exception to this is when you are the "expert witness" in the room and withholding your point of view would be inappropriate or obstructionist. By and large, in

decision-making meetings where the emotional and financial stakes are high, you will be more helpful to the family by positioning yourself as a neutral but helpful observer.

- *Formulate and test hypotheses (out loud).* Part of your role in being a facilitator is to play the part of the social scientist in the room, particularly in high-conflict situations. As a scientist, you will model the gathering of interpersonal and financial data, generating a reasonably testable question, and then formulate it in terms that family members can validate or invalidate.

   One example of this might occur around the formulation of investment policy for a family investment partnership, where there is an appearance of agreement but you are sensing a silent protest from one or more members. In the spirit of good scientific inquiry, you gather and mentally process emerging data you are seeing and hearing about interactions occurring. Then, you formulate a question for the group by synthesizing the publicly available data in the room, namely, the appearance of agreement in Jason, Ely, and Greg alongside an equally apparent uneasiness in Sherrie and Steven. The tone of your question is not judgmental, but genuinely curious questioning. You convey, like a good scientist, that you have a hypothesis that there is less agreement than meets the eye, and you do this in a way that signals that you are willing to be proven wrong. To invite participants to also "get scientific," I will sometimes even say explicitly that I am forming a hypothesis and ask them to help me sharpen it and assist in validating or disconfirming it. In the case of the investment policy discussion above, I might ask, "Can you see what might make me believe you are not all on the same page about this policy?"

- *Lead by example.* Model openness of inquiry and nonpartisan approaches to interpersonal exchanges. Let the family group experience firsthand the way superheated issues can be explored in a dispassionate but caring manner. Let them see honesty and integrity in action. When conflicts emerge, don't rush in to snuff out the polarization. Instead, convey trust that the family has within its means the ability to solve problems, even if not everything all at once.

- *Build small agreements.* Expert facilitation is not always marked by dramatic events and life-changing "ahas," but is often a product of bite-size resolutions that can be used as building blocks for a better functioning family. Unlike participants in the heat of argument, facilitators can listen for the one source of agreement amidst the 10 things just said, make explicit observations about those areas where there is agreement and ask if there are other such areas that can be found and built upon. On the other hand, don't make observations about agreements unless they really exist—acting like there is an agreement on the table when there isn't only injects artifice into the room and will postpone effective dealing with productive conflict.

- *Bring patience to the room.* Make sure that any overly ambitious agenda you have for the meeting is checked at the door. Meeting a family where they are and moving them forward at their pace is a hallmark of successful facilitation. All the preparation you've done is like leading the horse to water. The choice to drink is theirs. You are there to help but not to push when doing so is more about you than them.

- *Connect the dots.* Combine similar ideas that are brought to bear. Draw comparisons regarding what two people are saying. Look for patterns and linkages. If, for example, the family members assume the same roles when conflict arises in more than one instance, ask them if that is often the case in other spheres as well. In the investment policy example above, you might say that you've noticed that Sherrie and Steven seemed to go silent when they were talking about the new foundation charter as well and ask if that is a pattern that should be discussed. In another case, connecting the dots might mean pointing out common themes that seem to energize the family in a positive way.

- *Play the role not being played.* Is the group stuck? If so, many times the role of the facilitator is to play the role not being played in the group. This typically requires advance training but may take the form of choosing silence when everyone is talking over each other, or confrontation when everyone else is skirting an issue, or reflecting on someone's feelings when they appear overly masked by intellectualization. It can mean speaking the unspoken, often characterized as saying "the emperor has no clothes" or paying homage to the "elephant in the living room."

- *Track your own reactions; use them as data in the formulation of hypotheses.* As you've heard before, you are your best instrument, especially in facilitation situations. If you find you are reacting strongly to something going on, don't just react. Ask yourself what it is you are reacting to and what might be driving your reaction.

    If, for example, you find yourself falling asleep or getting bored, do not take these reactions at face value. These reactions are often related to overuse of defensive styles of intellectualization and denial. This means that if you find yourself disengaging this way, it may be because the family is in flight from some issue and using an overintellectualized discourse to mask a more important dynamic.

    Equally, if you find you are getting angry with someone, put the feeling through an introspective due diligence to pinpoint the origins of the anger. Anger is usually defensive, and often for facilitators, countertransferential, meaning that you are reacting to something related to what *you* bring to the situation more than what is called for in the situation. The earlier case where the advisor unconsciously overidentified with the son in the father–son dyad and then proceeded to act as if it were true is an example of not tracking well what is going on with you.

■ *Promote the kind of discussion that is needed.* Depending on what you are trying to accomplish, you can structure different types of discussions that open, narrow, or provide closure in conversations. If you want to *open up* the discursive field, brainstorm, free association, list, and survey techniques should be deployed. If you want to *narrow* the discussion, use techniques of polling, prioritization, eliminating duplicate options, and voting. If you wish to obtain *closure,* use negative polling (eliminate options to get to keepers), develop and apply decision criteria, or generate next steps as a way to close the current discussion out.

■ *Reflect it back.* You may be asked to weigh in on a matter in your role as facilitator. If you are genuinely in an expert position, you should weigh in. If the truth being sought is, in your opinion, resonant in the family, then reflect it back to them in the form of questions about what they think about the matter.

■ *Do the work until you can't.* One guiding principle I often use with family and work groups is that they should be left alone as long as they are doing the core tasks agreed upon. This approach to facilitation is based on a less-is-more model—as long as the group is working! When groups get stuck and/or veer from their core work, it almost never works to attempt to drive the family harder. Instead, when the work breaks down, the facilitation regimen shifts toward one where you are inquiring about what seems to be in the way of the work. Note that the question is not "why aren't you working?," which calls for causal judgments, but what is in the way, which calls for an analysis of whatever resistances are operative around the theme. If you can't get the work done, what is preventing it? Modeling this way of questioning the family's process will begin to teach them to do the same.

■ *What's going on? Assemble and reframe the fact pattern.* Often, one of the most interesting things a facilitator can ask when there is a lot of activity in the meeting is "what's going on?" This is a genuine question, and will usually stop a group in its tracks and provoke a discovery process that uncovers one or two core processes going on that are being masked by a frenzy of seemingly disconnected conversations and activity. The answer, "we don't know," may require that you assemble the fact pattern you have seen and reframe it as a stimulus to get the family to work harder on what may be really going on.

These items should help to orient you toward the basics of facilitation. Chapter 8 will help you with other steps you can take to perfect your craft and build confidence that you can run a range of meeting types that vary in their tilt toward either content- or process-centric designs.

## Family Meeting Worst Nightmares

No chapter on family meetings would be complete if it did not go to the heart of the things that keep advisors up at night with respect to anticipated family meetings. There are a handful of situations that no advisor, however experienced, would want to see happen in a family meeting context. These situations can usually be described in the following basic cases, and go beyond mere agenda deviations, presentation technology failures, passive resistance, or minor ground rule violations. They are difficult situations, hands-down. While each advisor may have his or her own worst nightmare scenario, they tend to cluster around certain types of occurrences. In most cases, there are things you can do that are worth thinking about in advance. The following provides the means for you to prepare yourself for certain possibilities and some rules of thumb as to how you can respond should they happen:

- *Escalating conflict.* While the meeting may have started off smoothly enough, in this scenario the emotional valences surrounding discussion themes become far stronger than expected. Even if you have prepared participants well and understand what the central issues are, families will often use the safety of your presence unconsciously to intensify their reactions. The intensity of the live encounter can surprise the advisor. This happened to one advisor in a discussion with a family business regarding matters of compensation for family members in the business. What started as a calm discussion of the current state of affairs became increasingly combative when it came time to determine criteria for changes to compensation. Even good preparation could not mitigate this possibility.

  Rule of thumb: *Identify the emerging conflict and use the group to clarify what it is about. Once the outlines of the conflict are identified, shift away from the conflict per se and toward the development of a process and criteria by the group by which it would like to use to reach resolution. This is an explicit intervention on the most basic levels of governance process and will promote in the family a reframing of the process and lessen the immediate severity of the conflict. Conflicts that are not central to the purpose of the meeting should be relegated to the "parking lot" and flagged for further work.*

- *Silences.* In some cases, the worst fear of an advisor running a family meeting is that the family will close down in silence at key moments in the meeting. Silences present ambiguous stimuli that often call out anxiety in observers. High-energy advisors don't always handle silences well and feel that they have to be filled at all cost. One advisor finished a presentation of a proposed estate planning scenario only to be met by a stone-cold silence. Her tension hit the ceiling because she assumed that the silence represented a palpable disapproval of her proposal.

> Rule of thumb: *Normally, there are two kinds of silence in a family group: working or productive silences, and nonworking, nonproductive silences. The initial approach you take to each is the same; namely, let it happen. Productive silences often follow a powerful insight or "aha" moment related to something significant that has just occurred. Within reason, these silences should be left alone because they are about the incorporation and digestion of new learning. The difference in approach changes if the silence is unproductive, in which case your approach after a short period of time will be to simply ask what is going on? Someone will then say, "we've all gone silent," and you will simply ask in response, "what do you make of that?" or "what sense are you giving the silence?" In general, you do not want to bail a group out of its silence by jumping in yourself unless it makes clear strategic sense.*

- *Domineering person, the interpersonal bully.* Groups generate speaking contests by their very nature, however subtle or pronounced. A persistent, one-sided contest almost invariably will degrade the process and produce blowback when it is time to actually make a decision—sometimes in the form of passive-aggressive resistance. Better to address it early and often if it is a preexisting tendency in the family.

> Rule of thumb: *Intervene by either calling aggressively on others to respond and speak their minds and/or by directing feedback to the offending party. This feedback can be delivered by pointing out that "while you seem to have a lot of valuable things to say, we really need to hear from others." Many times, this is enough because it draws formal attention to the process of speaking over the group and the passive submission to it by other participants. Sometimes, you can deliver the message in a comedic way, which may make the intervention more palatable to a group who may be otherwise quite anxious around dealing with the issues head-on.*

- *Crying.* Fewer issues unnerve a novice facilitator more than when someone breaks into tears. This will hardly be a rare occurrence, though, as you will deal with some clients for whom crying comes easier than others and with issues of substance enough to be potentially painful.

Sometimes there will be tears of relief, when you've done something right.

> Rule of thumb: *As with many potentially overdetermined events, crying may have several origins and be overcoded with many meanings by those in audience. This means you should be prepared to both provide a safe space for crying to occur and pay attention to the reactions of the group. Usually, the group's reaction will let you know whether crying from this specific person is unusual or standard fare. If tears are in play for anything other than legitimate sadness or grief, others' reactions will clue you in to how focused you should become to the distress in the room. Don't under- or overreact while trying to ascertain the purpose of the tears and whether they are achieving their purpose or finding resistance or irritation in others. As people react, ask them what it is they are reacting to, besides the obvious. Usually, they will tell you and supply you with the history of crying and what its intended and unintended effects have typically been.*

- *Walking out of the meeting.* Ideally, you will have vetted the family enough to know that they are healthy enough to manage themselves through a meeting without flying apart at the seams. However, you may still find yourself running a meeting where someone feels they have to bolt. In a discussion among several family members and trustees about changing investment advisors for the trusts for two adult children, one of the kids burst into tears and stormed out of the room, leaving a semistunned audience. She had developed a strong attachment to the investment advisor and was very upset at the rationale being given for making the change. For many advisors, this is not an unthinkable type of occurrence.

> Rule of thumb: *Often, the initial reaction of a family group from which a member has bolted is to act as if nothing just happened. Depending on how dramatic the exit, conversation may continue on or come to a halt. Usually, the first role of the facilitator is to direct the group's attention to it. If no one does so spontaneously, direct someone to go find the person, starting with the person you think will have the best chance of bringing the person back. You can ask the group about what they think happened and whether it has happened before. They will usually offer up both their perspective on whether this is typical or atypical and what it means to each of them. When the person returns, you can extend the same inquiry if others don't while trying to understand the forces in play that might have led to the departure. Do not drop your stance of compassionate curiosity, as it will serve you well in this circumstance as in others.*

## Tips and Takeaways for the New Financial Advisor

The key message to you is that you can do family meetings. While there are some circumstances that dictate the use of outside facilitation assistance—as when there are high content and process, or more pure process outcomes, being sought—you can get better at this. Your ability to know when to stage such meetings and how to execute them will grow with practice and with supervision and feedback from peers.

There is much to consider when running family meetings. Good preparation with respect to goal and objective development and meeting design can go a long way toward engineering a highly effective service event. A well-run family meeting, even if you zigzag to the perfect outcome, serves to improve family financial decision making and your standing as a servant of positive change in the family. As you continue to plan and participate in family meetings, you will get better and your design and execution confidence will grow. You will strengthen your role opposite the family and often avoid numerous false starts and wasted encounters.

Rather than having potentially suspicious stakeholders around work you do that is cloaked in mystery, you introduce new forms of transparency into the family system in measured doses. You will democratize family decision making and, as a result, set the stage for greater participation and buy-in to family wealth solutions. You may also lose your status as the "enemy" working with Mom and Dad and gain entrée to the next generation of wealth holders, which can in itself further annuitize your business.

To summarize, make sure you:

- *Over- rather than underprepare for family meetings.* Try to get to everyone at least by phone in advance and make sure you know what they are bringing as agendas to the meeting. Make sure you organize venue and logistics to support meeting objectives.
- *Execute good meetings by staying with the agenda, while paying attention to the dynamic components that can support or undermine the agenda.* Send the signal that you have heard the various issues that could be brought up but are going to focus on those that support the current objectives. Use of techniques like placing issues on "parking lots"—separate lists of issues warranting further follow up—can support the family's ability to stay on track.

*(Continued)*

■ *A strong message is sent to the family when you provide good follow-through once the meeting has adjourned.* You can counteract the inertia that can follow even excellent meetings by checking in with participants and nudging them along in taking the next steps.

Having addressed the device of family meetings, we can now turn to some of the kinds of life events you may encounter with your family clients. Use of family meetings can be a key component of your strategy in work with families facing the kinds of transitions we will now review.

# CHAPTER 6

# Major Life Events

## *How You Can Help Families Navigate Difficult Times*

A core reason clients come to you is to help them prepare for a range of changing circumstances, from retirement and college funding to funding for disability and death. Reacting well to planned and unplanned transitions can position you well to enable your families to benefit in ways that are invaluable. Yet this is often easier said than done, even for individuals who are highly trained to facilitate family well-being. Many of the tools you are familiar with will be helpful. For example, financial scenario planning is an extremely valuable service to provide for families. In this way, you help them anticipate the ups and downs of markets and other variables and how these can support or undermine clients' navigation of developmental or catastrophic events.

However, this chapter is *not* principally about doing a better job of financial scenario modeling; it *is* about what actually happens when the wheels come off, when something very big and (potentially) very bad is happening in the life of a family, even if what is happening is *normal*. This means we are addressing how you behave and react in the context of events such as death, divorce, and disability, the sale of a business, or the arrival of a financial windfall. You once again have the option to be helpful to families in unexpected ways, or as we have seen, to make yourself irrelevant or even unhelpful. You can help them establish a navigational beacon or simply hope to keep selling them goods and services through the vicissitudes of the oncoming transition. The opportunity may not always be there in the same way for each client system, but it is in these circumstances where your impact has the potential to be profound and lasting.

To help you react to the challenges and seize the opportunities presented in your role as the new financial advisor, we will develop a transition framework through which one can view the various transitions that present themselves, as well as delve more specifically into those related to death, retirement, divorce, sale of a business, substance abuse problems, mental illness, and end-of-life transitions. While far from exhaustive, these representative situations together help advisors better orient themselves and their practices to the many and varied events that their clients will experience.

## Transition Framework

It would require much hubris on my part to imagine it possible to convey how to help even small human systems navigate substantial transitions in a short chapter. It is not only that in many cases these transitions can require deep expertise in support of resolution; it is also the case that the experts don't themselves completely agree on what constitutes good help. As a result, the goals that I suggest are framed in modest terms and oriented toward incremental improvements in how you help your client-families ride out complicated times and, at a minimum, avoid becoming part of the problem or a drag on the system as it attempts to change.

### Time in Transitions

In the simplest way, transitions have a beginning, middle, and usually a series of partial resolutions that set the stage for the writing of the family's next chapter. The kinds of transitions we are focused on don't really "end" per se any more than working through the death of a family member ends. They transform. They do this in what Jay Hughes would call a "viral" way, whether positively or negatively. In other words, they generate various sequelae or mutations that either positively support the family's evolution or accelerate its entropic descent.

Transitions also involve two types of time, which, for simplicity, I will call *clock time* and *psychological time.*

> *Clock time* is the time most advisors pay attention to and around which most financial products are tied. Insurance policies, trusts, and asset allocations play out in clock time. Clock time is that time measured by years, months, hours, and minutes. It is mathematical. It is a peculiar human invention that runs its linear course with an almost inhuman disregard of its inventors' attempts to cheat its logic. This kind of time chases us and marches us inexorably toward death, even as psychological time deconstructs linearity and bends clock time to its fantastical purposes.
>
> *Psychological time* is time that says grown men may act like 10-year-olds, that 18 months postdivorce is too soon to begin dating again,

and that painful childhood events can drive the formation of experiential templates extending decades beyond their historical origin. In a word, psychological time does not care what time it is. A minute on your watch can seem an eternity under the right circumstances. Psychological time runs on its own asynchronous logic, cutting and pasting experience into montages of old and new. Psychological time is memorialized in language and discourse. Its only content is what has passed. In Heidegger's terms, it is this past that presents us with the possibility of the future and with the inevitability of our mortality.

The death of a family member often dramatizes the often asynchronous relationship these two types of time have with one another, with the law dictating sets of definitive steps that must be completed within certain time frames, regardless of the family's psychological readiness to process certain kinds of information alongside its trajectory of grief. These are instances in which advisor stewardship can have a tremendously positive effect by working to coordinate these two timelines with one another and honoring the pacing that psychological time requires.

## Types of Events and Transitions

Another consideration concerning the transition framework is to focus on event types and the associated approach or orientation that can be taken. Figure 6.1 illustrates what is meant by this along the lines of event emergence and scope. Events we are concerned with include those that are anticipated and unanticipated and affect either specific client systems or broader groups of clients.

The planned retirement of a specific patriarch might exemplify an anticipated event affecting a specific family. The approach to this emphasizes preventive measures, taking into account the financial, familial, and psychological realities that loom on the horizon. Having a large book of 50- to 65-year-old baby boomers in your practice represents another anticipated event affecting broader client segments and requires prevention measures of a more programmatic nature. Equally, the "untimely" death of a family member is a highly specific and unanticipated event requiring different stewardship through and beyond the crisis, while a significant market implosion or larger catastrophe requires agile communication and educational capabilities. The focus of this chapter by and large is on those events that affect individual client systems, though in some cases extrapolation to broader client segment events will be touched upon as well.

Each transition an advisor works with has its very specific characteristics and implications. Within the transition framework used here, it becomes

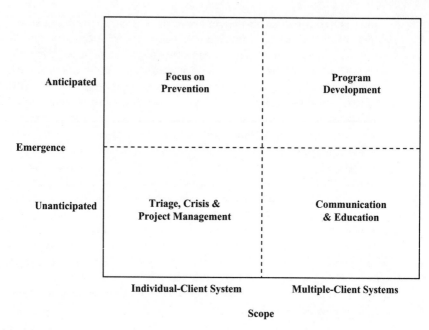

FIGURE 6.1  Transition Event Types and Approach

important to step back and analyze transitions according to the themes they present, the timelines in which they can be expected to play out, the role the new financial advisor can play, and the potential implications for service delivery.

- *Themes*. As the history of the event unfolds, it usually is articulated in themes carried on a more or less coherent narrative. Some themes might encompass "growing up," or "shifting from entrepreneur to financial steward," or "moving from married to single in midlife." Sometimes, helping clients identify these themes can help to normalize what they are going through and make them feel less isolated. It can give them distance and perspective, without trivializing the scope of what they are going through.
- *Timelines*. As we've discussed previously, the passage of time is hardly straightforward for the human animal. For individuals in transition, time can seem bottomless. In part, this is because we are often very impatient, especially when fear, pain, grief, or hurt is involved. Sometimes it is important to look, however, at how long in clock time things tend to last. One client I worked with was increasingly impatient with his spouse, who had lost her son (his stepson) three years previously. His

feeling was that it was time to get over it already. It took several occasions of saying that he should think of her grieving timeline in terms of decades, not years, to give him comfort that something was not going really wrong with her and their relationship. So it is important to "clock" transitions in normative terms without getting rigid about when something should be "over."

- *Role considerations.* These considerations concern issues informing the advisor's stance opposite the transition—you will not play the same role across all transitions over and beyond the deep listening and care that is de rigueur in this new advisory world. In some cases, you will play a very active technical role, whereas in others you may play much more of an organizing or managerial role. In still others, you may simply "hold the hands" of your clients and interact with the more emotional dimensions of the transition, with other advisors taking the lead. This can happen during, for example, the sale of a business where the family wealth manager takes a back seat to an investment banker in the *transaction* but plays a prominent role in the *transition*.

- *Service implications.* The kinds of services above and beyond the usual that might come into play may vary across transition types as well and, for the new financial advisor, are tilted toward any plausible support for human capital interventions. Depending on the transition, your service model and approach may have to change. As the realities of divorce or retirement or sudden wealth set in, what service and even marketing opportunities emerge? If, for example, you find you are dealing with a number of women facing divorce, can you envision creating new educational and even networking opportunities that enable these women to more ably navigate this transition and do so in less isolation?

Several event types are are summarized in Table 6.1 with respect to themes you might expect, how long their associated transitions might be expected to take, roles the new financial advisor can assume, and potential service implications that might follow. Each of the events and themes summarized in the table is discussed in more detail through the balance of this chapter.

## Death of a Patriarch or Matriarch

When a patriarch or matriarch passes on, the short-term differences between whether the death was more or less expected will wash out with respect to the unfolding transition. There are some differences with respect to whether the death was violent, accidental, or the result of a prolonged illness, but drilling further into these variations is beyond the scope of the new financial

TABLE 6.1  Summary of Events Signaling Important Client Transitions

| Event | Themes | Timelines | Role Considerations | Service Implications |
|---|---|---|---|---|
| Death of a patriarch/matriarch | Grief; power vacuum; new regime formation | 2–4 years | Orchestration of technical requirements with family milestones | Family meetings; advisor/service provider management; project management; scenario planning |
| Retirement | Definition of "next chapter"; role shifts; legacy and generativity | 1–3 years | Vocational identity elicitation; story and legacy development | Couple meetings; legacy archives; transition planning and funding |
| Divorce | Grief and loss; "what about the kids"; harm mitigation and exacerbation; asset decathexis | 2–4 years | Who's the client? Managing allegiances; maintenance of orthogonality | Empowerment education; scenario development; estate and legacy revisions |
| Sale of a business/family business | Meaning of sale; legacy; loss; career development; becoming "rich," new identity development | 1–4 years | Approach to sale (objectivity); advisor role shifts around new form of assets; increased prominence of your role and services | Pre- and postscenario development; career development services; family office development; estate development; philanthropic planning |
| Death of a child | Extreme grief; survivor guilt; shifting values and identity | 5–15 years | Your grief and countertransference; service provider orchestration | Custom planning and scenario development; project management |
| Mental illness and substance abuse | Role changes; deception; danger; fear; false starts | 1–10 years | Treatment resource options awareness; empathy for system damage | Project management; educational services |
| Elder care transitions | Role reversals; final chapter development; care-giving systems | 4–10 years | Coaching for caregivers; attention to shifting obligations among system participants | Educational seminars; resource and referral development |

advisor's treatment. Suffice it to say that the death of a patriarch or matriarch, who is usually someone in position of leadership, is different because of role attributes developed during his or her reign.

## Grief

With some room for variation, a positive outcome to this transition will directly correlate with the extent to which the family has been meeting around the topic, and has had some opportunity to articulate with each other what should happen in the event of the patriarch or matriarch's death. Put in the simplest terms, if the family has been meeting and planning for this eventuality, it stands a stronger chance of mitigating negative viral consequences. I spoke earlier of the need to coordinate the two timelines that commence upon death—the legal/juridical timeline (clock) and the psychological timeline (running an elliptical grief cycle)—and the need to synchronize their relationship.

Though one can never really synchronize the "planned death" with its actual occurrence in either legal or emotional terms, early attempts to coordinate these sequences pay dividends on the back end. For example, it is one thing to preview and document all the legal processes that attend a death, and another to build in processes for the family to meet with each other beyond the required funeral circumstances and separately with legal advisors that are explicitly *not* about estate settlement per se. This means that the first meeting after the funeral should not in most cases be the reading of the will. The chief resistance around doing this kind of planning while the individual is alive will often be the difficulty family members have in bringing up the need for such meetings. The adult children will have a range of worries, some superstitious (e.g., if you bring something up, you'll make it happen) and some defensive (e.g., not wanting to appear greedy).

This is where the financial advisor can have significant positive influence. Regardless of whether death is on the visible horizon due to an illness, everyone I know is going to die. This means that the opportunity to gently press the family into meetings about the technical and familial aspects of the eventual death of the patriarch or matriarch can be a tremendous help to the family's long-term viability with each other. One of the biggest errors advisors make here, too, is to have these meetings only with the client couple. While this may be helpful to the surviving spouse, it really does nothing for the next generation and does not mitigate what will become a likely second round of grieving when the surviving spouse sees the children polarize in unnecessary ways.

In addition, just as there are two timelines set in motion at death, there are two derivative sets of role types that track these two temporal flows. One individual or subset of individuals will orient themselves toward the juridical tasks that have to be accomplished in clock time and will become what seem to the others as taskmasters charging ahead with their overt forms of grieving in suspension. This set of family members will appear to overfunction with regard to getting things done, both to the relief and sometimes consternation of the other set, who instead take up the more overt aspects of grieving. This latter group's experience of loss will be palpable to themselves and others. They may appear to underfunction and may need to be propped up through the early phases of loss and grief.

If someone in the system or associated with it isn't helping them understand these role variations as more or less normal and preparing all for grieving as an evolutionary process where each will go through a certain set of phases, trouble may lie ahead. The overfunctioning taskmasters, because of their need to anchor on the legal timelines, can be later perceived as having railroaded certain decisions over the more vulnerable, grieving members. Decisions that may have already been made in predeath planning will be second-guessed and the motives of the taskmasters questioned. Assuming the motives aren't in fact sinister, guilt around what happened will emerge for the taskmaster and will begin to stir a toxic brew of emotions that often congeals into anger and defensiveness. From here, the seeds of familial alienation are freshly fertilized and the defensive style hardened.

## Power Vacuum

Further challenges that attend this particular kind of death relate to the power vacuum that is created. Whether consciously planned or not, a new regime will begin to evolve, and it will either evolve along positive and inclusive or Machiavellian lines. As alluded to earlier, if one of the taskmasters will also be the one moving into the new power vacancy, they can often expect a resistant constituency, so the style by which the new leader emerges can be a focus of the advisor's coaching through the transition. To a large extent, the new leader's style will evolve in relationship to the level and type of identification the new leader has with his parent. If the parent was a dictator, for example, the child will have developed a relationship to that style that incorporates or rejects various elements of that leadership paradigm. As with most character formation, this emergent character has been in unconscious rehearsal of this script for years, making any intervention on it a delicate matter. One thing is clear: the advisor will be in no position to affect this if they have become so caught up in the needs of the parents that they have not early on begun to develop a relationship with the kids. The probability that the adult children will work with an advisor they first meet at the reading of the will hovers near zero. This means that the advisor should always begin a relationship with the children during the client on-boarding and discovery processes or as soon thereafter as possible.

## Regime Change

What complicates the normal grieving process (see Figure 6.2) in this case is the additional emotional contours associated with regime change. Those (adult) kids that were protected under the previous regime become increasingly exposed and vulnerable now that a long-resentful sibling has ascended to the throne. Even in financial abundance, a new sense of privation can occur in some and fighting can break out over what appears to outsiders as trivia (recall the cathexis made to assets and other [valuable] objects discussed earlier).

This means that the advisor should understand that different individuals in the family will arc through the grieving process at different speeds and in relationship to each other. For example, as the history of sibling relationships shows, each will orient himself to the others through a process of differentiation. The implication is that if one sibling is angrier than another in his initial orientation to the death, others will assume emotional postures that are different from this (sadness, hurt, guilt) and can be expected to pass through an angry phase later. The advisor can play a small part in

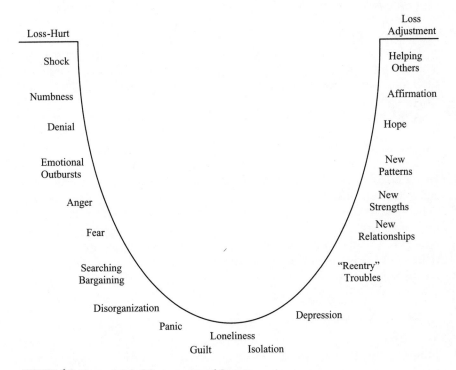

FIGURE 6.2 Normal Grief Processes and Stages

normalizing for the clients the fact that they will proceed at varying speeds through this transition and should try to understand each other's differing realities rather than see them harden into deep resentments and relational breakdowns. Statements like, "yes, your sister is very angry now but parts of that are normal and will pass, as long as we do our best to let her express these feelings and don't back her into decisions that shouldn't get made now," convey that you are not alarmed by what is happening and—within reason—neither should he be either.

As a financial advisor, you cannot be expected to play family therapist here any more than in other instances, and it is not often the case that grieving families will march themselves into a therapists office and tee themselves up for grief counseling anyway. Your stance can, however, be one that instead recognizes both the way in which specific family members may be careening through the grief cycle themselves and the ways in which each individual plays off of the others. You can provide empathic responses to each individually and nudge the family, where possible, away from making big decisions when the emotional valences are extreme. Clients can be educated. Their experiences can be normalized (e.g., "I would be more worried about you if you weren't feeling some of this."), and your stance can represent a steady attention to both the financial and familial impact, while privileging the latter over the former when in doubt. The core challenge of managing the two time frames is that they are often at cross purposes, making the family make the biggest decisions precisely when they may be least equipped to do so. There is no neat formula here, but buying time for the family to process its grief is often the prudent course of facilitation for the advisor.

## Retirement

Fewer social stages are as in flux and culture specific as retirement. And "planning for retirement" is one of the dominant templates underlying the delivery of financial services. This treatment of retirement assumes a general understanding of the laws of savings and the massively successful (for the mutual fund industry in particular) legislation of mental accounting around retirement assets. Here, what is critical is what the notion of retirement really means rather than how it is funded.

### Image versus Reality

As a stage of life, there is the retirement articulated by the retail investment companies in television ads and the one that is actually anticipated and unfolds along very personal lines. It is, for many, the penultimate chapter of life, with the final chapter about deterioration and death. Like a Rorschach inkblot, it is something onto which much is projected that is often both exciting and fearful. Often, the retirement project involves deconstructing these very projections and reformulating them in highly specific terms. It is not only about the difficulty of writing this next, difficult chapter; it is about how this gets done given that the protagonist's role has to be reinvented outside the dominant, usually work-related systems, on which the individual's identity was built. Clearly, one retires only in relationship to something, and that is usually work. And it is here that a shedding of one identity and the emergence of another unfolds in a more or less generative way. Even as this old identity comes to an end, the ultimate end is increasingly difficult to deny. Retirement then becomes less about building a brand new identity cycle than in architecting an identity that is provisional and vulnerable.

## Identity and Role Changes as a Family Affair

Often, the first and most powerful message from society, family stakeholders, and the individual contemplating retirement is: "How is he or she going to stay busy?" Professionals will often be distracted by this, and believe their mission with the target retiree is to collude with this busy-ness agenda and throw gasoline on the fire. In fact, there are many reasons to intervene in countervailing ways, principally those related to the major developmental tasks that are emerging. Among these is the question of what retirement *means* to the individual and the surrounding stakeholders. For example, is retirement:

- An extension of one's greater vocation (from the Latin *vocare,* to call, as in calling)?
- A parking place where the individual is to be anesthetized with "leisure" activities, the more the merrier?
- A time to punch the ticket on experiences not had?
- A time to give back to society or to one's children/grandchildren?
- An illusory category that enables one to come back and disrupt what has been left behind (Sonnenfeld's "general," the departing executive who is forever plotting his return and who will only really depart in a coffin)?
- A time for creativity and generativity?

For stakeholders, is retirement:

- A relief (in, say, nonfamily executives in the family business)?
- A loss (as in, for example, the same nonfamily executives)?

- A coming intrusion (as where, for example, the spouse has built a perfectly satisfying life in parallel, thank you)?
- Foreshadowing of death and infirmity?
- An opportunity to reconnect?

It is not surprising, then, that as in all matters of wealth management this one, too, has a number of moving parts. Experience suggests that there is a range of glide paths that can be taken on the way to landing the retirement agenda. As shown in Figure 6.3, each has different implications for the approach the financial advisor takes. Only in the upper right-hand quadrant, where high clarity about the coming chapter is married with a positive valence, is the advisor left in the comfort zone of providing traditional planning and investment services. For individuals in this quadrant, you are cast in the role of a traditional support player in actualizing well-articulated plans and fantasies—the stuff of airbrushed ads.

Many do not enter the period this way and have multiple internal and external attachments that are difficult to unravel. Once again, the advisor has an opportunity to be part of a cacophony of voices worried about the expediency with which the retiree can be slotted into a new and busy

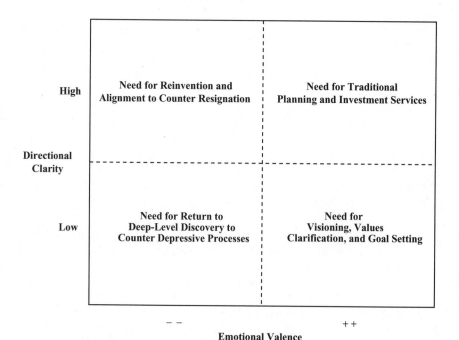

FIGURE 6.3 Differing Glide Paths into Retirement

retirement lifestyle or to move into a more Socratic dialogue with the individual and the family about what is at stake, what is going on, and what it means for all system participants. This requires less skill than courage to play the role that is probably not being played opposite the client system, namely, to raise deep questions about what is really desired in this next chapter called retirement.

Positive framing is thus important here, but not to the extent that there is an obfuscation of the forces that are simply pushing the person out to pasture. Knowing that roles and identities will be changing in all participants in relationship to the retiree is critical in helping your client understand all the forces at work and constituents to understand. Does the retiree want to reengage the left-behind family at just the developmental moment that the family is on to other tasks and geographies? This is especially important in the case where retirement is from a complex system, such as a family business or family office, where it is not enough to give "two weeks' notice" and let the cards fall where they may. As ever, the advisor who has gotten in and developed alliances with these family and nonfamily stakeholders is the one who will be the depth player through this transition as well as others.

The key message here is to take thoughtful positions opposite the varying components of the retirement transition—the mix of real constraints and fantastical issues associated with Madison Avenue's commoditization of retirement, as well as the reconfiguration of role identity in the individual's work and family system. The key trap to avoid is simple collusion with all the social and cultural assumptions about what retirement is about. For many, living out a stereotyped retirement will in fact be the path they travel—that's why there are stereotypes: they fit for many of us. Where the road is bumpy or where desires deviate from the map that has been given is where you stand to become helpful as a conavigator through this important transition.

## Divorce

It would seem safe to say that if the divorce rate in the United States averages between 40 and 50 percent, you stand a significant chance of seeing this transition ripple through your practice. Divorce is almost always a complex matter with well-known issues such as infidelity and breakdowns in communications, shared expectations and parenting practices. It is not unusual for money issues to be front and center, thus again presenting the new financial advisor with a number of challenges and opportunities. Of all the possible themes, those discussed below can have relatively direct implications for how you retain business through the divorce transition.

## Reorganizing Alliances

As with any transition, there is a beginning, a middle, and a set of resolutions that will play out through time. During the beginning phases, the advisor may or may not become aware of what is going on between the couple. If the advisor does become aware, it presents them with their first challenge in the form of whom they are going to form an alliance with—something you have typically not had to face until now. Even in the most "amicable" divorce scenario, it is highly perilous to take a side early in the game. As conflicts around money are often a substantial driver of divorces in the first place, one thing that is clear is that through the process of divorce, money issues do not decrease in importance. This is true both with respect to the real uptick in expenses associated with doubling the households and with the symbolic values associated with dividing the estate and its income streams and assets.

In addition, each participant in the couple will be sorting who in their social universe is on their side, who is neutral (if any), and who is on the other person's side, as will be members of their social universe doing this to them. This means that where you play will be a function of where you are being placed by each member of the couple and where you are placing yourself. Referring to the earlier maxim of knowing yourself says that understanding your reactions to the separation and divorce emerging in front of you will be among your first orders of business.

- Do you want one of the clients over another?
- How do you see the parties (who has been wronged; who is the perpetrator)?
- Do you feel you could continue to provide services to both parties as separate client systems?
- How do you feel about how the children are being treated by each of the parties?

You will not do your best work if these and related questions are not sufficiently sorted in your mind. You also need to prepare yourself for the more likely eventuality that you will end up with one or the other side and that it might not be the one you want to end up with.

## Is It All about the Money?

The courts usually have their own default formulas for dividing up the marital estate and assigning alimony (tax deductible to the payor and income to the payee) and child support. Attorneys may fan or occasionally quell any financial conflagration that erupts in the process, and your role may be highly constricted in this context. Because of the associated emotional and financial complexities, this is not a bad thing for most advisors, who would soon find themselves in way over their head in this superheated environment.

The implication for most advisors around divorce will be that they keep a steady, orthogonal relationship to both parties and to lay out for both parties both your policies in relationship to separating couples and your services that relate to postdivorce financial planning, the latter being an extremely important service. Your ability to be empathic to both sides and not collude (in most cases) with the demonization of the one over the other should be driven by the assumption that in the interior of most marital relationships, it usually does take two to tango—and to dismantle a marriage. In most cases, another component of this approach is to keep an eye on the children and try to help the parents draw this feature of what is going on into the foreground of what they are doing. In most cases, supporting the intention of one parent to vengefully drive the other into financial poverty does not serve the interests of the children.

Postdivorce financial modeling offers a powerful tool for the rearticulation of the client's values and to have categories—such as financial and developmental intentions related to the children—at a front-and-center position in financial line items. Inasmuch as divorce will also often follow the "grief" curve, your empathic approach to postdivorce planning should be sensitive to the "phase" the person is in but can also help tip the psychodynamic balance toward the "adaptation" side of the arc. Reasonably clear scenario planning can act as a healing tool that is unavailable to a psychotherapist and others who are supporting each through the process. Deep financial uncertainty aggravates progress through this transition and your behavior as a trusted advisor in this context can lay the groundwork for a much deepened client relationship.

To summarize:

- Sort your own reactions.
- Do stay orthogonal; don't prematurely take sides.
- When possible, elevate the issue of the kids.
- Do be empathetic.
- Don't—except under special circumstances—help to do what the courts and attorneys will do around estate resolution.
- Do frame your services in postseparation and postdivorce terms to give one or both a window into the other side of the transition.

## Sale of a Business

Few transitions have been as poorly understood by wealth managers as the sale of a business. Until recently, many advisors focused on the management of liquid wealth have misconstrued the sale of a business as a singularly positive event. However, unless the individual is a serial entrepreneur with a low-level cathexis to the business asset, this transition can be among the most destabilizing on the list. Even the experience of a death of a loved one does not usually result in as radical a change in the makeup of one's daily life, whose dominant hours are spent in the business.

## Ambivalence and Loss

In my experience as a financial advisor, the importance of this event is elevated because of a few interrelated reasons:

- The owner is highly cathected to the asset.
- The sale is a transition that looks dynamically more like a loss than a gain—something often completely reversed in the mind of the advisor.
- The destabilization and reconstruction of identity—tied as it is to role—is the core developmental challenge faced by the client (and often the client's family if it is a family business).

Simplistic constructs, like getting "cold feet" going into a transaction or having "seller's remorse" on the back end, do not convey the often profound nature of what is at stake. There are often deep ambivalences in play when business owners stare into the sale of their "baby," and it can be in part the new financial advisor's role to help the business owner and/or his or her family sort these out. For example, the promise of liquidity can be shadowed by the sheer vacancy of insight around what the owner(s) will do after the business is gone.

On the front end, the meaning of the sale—whether the sale is long planned for or the product of the surprise offer that is "too good to refuse"—can give significant shape to how this transition is launched, as can the circumstance under which the sale is undertaken—under duress or backed into because of the lack of a familial successor. As in the case of the retirement challenge, these antecedent conditions give shape to the sense of efficacy and control business owners have over the transaction, but will not obviate the need to conceptualize this as a transition that, to a greater or lesser extent, has an element of *loss* at its center.

## The Sale as a Family Affair

It is, of course, one thing to provide advice in this context when it involves an individual business owner and another when it involves several members of a family. In the latter case, several questions should be on the mind of the new financial advisor:

- How is each individual attached or cathected to the business whether they work in it or not?
- How are proceeds expected to be divided up and what are the messages attending this anticipated division?

- What next-phase considerations are in place and how articulated are they for each (for some it's a retirement transition; for others, a career stopper; etc.)?
- What decision-making processes led up to the sale (inclusive, democratic; unilateral, exclusive)?
- How are these processes expected to extend beyond the sale?
- What is anticipated in the way of family unity? What integrating and disintegrating processes are being set in motion?

Notice how little these questions have to do with postliquidity investment policy, risk tolerance, and asset allocation—the very things most financial advisors lead with in this circumstance. Make no mistake: these are important items to sort across the asset pools that will be created after the sale. They are usually nowhere near top-of-mind concerns in the client system, however, whose collective and individual identities may well be in play. One individual who sold a substantial business dropped off a crate containing about 150 investment management proposals that sped his direction when the announcement of the sale hit the presses. He asked that we try to "see if there are any differences among them. I can't tell them apart." A quick deconstruction of the pitch books confirmed rather than refuted this business owner's experience. The basic processes of goal setting, assessment of risk tolerance, asset allocation, and portfolio implementation were ticked off like clockwork in each presentation. For this family business steward, these books shared in a self-referential banality that bore little in relationship to what he and his family were going through, which included, among other things, the need to sort through substantial philanthropic and venture capital agendas.

The need, in Jay Hughes's terms, for the "transaction to support the transition" could not be more pronounced than in the sale of a family business. Groups like Tiger 21, the Institute for Private Investors, and the Family Office Exchange can in many cases provide safe harbor for former entrepreneurs and their families to gain insight and build new skills and identities in peer group environments. Though organized around the more technical aspects of wealth, these groups often have a component of their programming oriented toward the "transitional" dimensions of this historic event for the family.

## Death of a Child

It should be clear by now that much of what we are examining here of life events and transitions involves some form of loss, adaptation, and reinvention. The death of a child presents an extreme test of the idea that grief can take a normal course and that adaptation and reinvention are even possible. There are few things that come close to the devastation that this can cause and the level of bereavement can seem bottomless. "The grief caused by their child's death is not only painful but profoundly disorienting—children are not supposed to die."[1] Parental grief can

> ... *include an overwhelming sense of its magnitude, a sense that the pain will last forever, a sense that the grief is etched into one's very being. [Experts] explain that it is also important for these parents to express their anger outwardly so that it will not turn inward and possibly become a destructive force in the future. These specialists say that although there are many commonalities in parental grief, individual reactions often vary and that the same person may even experience contradictory reactions. They also say that the two responses experienced most commonly by bereaved parents are a baffling sense of disorientation and a deep conviction that they must never let go of the grief.*[2]

## Too Difficult for Words

Financial advisors, of course, have limited ability to affect the course of grief and bereavement in such profound circumstances, and so the approach again is to make sure that you are at least not part of the problem or find yourself in collusion with the forces that may degrade your clients' condition.

As I've advised many times before, your own reactions—and your defenses around these reactions—are the place to start. Being with someone having this level of grief will often engender in advisors an inability to talk about the loss of the child at all. The least effective approach is to act as if nothing has happened and that business can go on as usual, followed by only cursory acknowledgement of the death. Parents in these circumstances need to express their feelings and to know that they are heard. They do not need to be fixed or encouraged to cheer up. They already feel a tremendous sense of being robbed and cheated in ways that place a barrier between them and the people around them. Your willingness to sit with them, hear them and not be in a hurry may mean all the difference. The new journey they've been forcibly sent on will be measured in decades, even a lifetime. They will be reconfiguring their life among other people and resorting their relationships into those who are understanding and those whose own anxieties and defenses disable their ability to be part of this difficult journey. You can be part of the former group or the latter in large measure to the extent you are able to just be with the person.

You can also:

- Invite the parents to tell stories about the child.
- Inquire about how the other children are doing.
- Ask how they are doing.

- Inquire about whether they are getting the help they need regarding everything from household matters to financial matters.
- Locate a local support group for grieving parents and refer them to it when they are ready to hear it and not as a way to shove the grief out of your office.
- Convey that there is no hurry for them to "get on with their lives."
- Tell them there is no one way to go through this but that they needn't go through it alone.
- Shed a tear with them if you are so moved.
- Acknowledge birthdates and anniversaries.
- Remind them that healing is not about forgetting.
- Let them know that they will get through this in time, that it is hard work, that they should be patient and that you are prepared to be *very* patient with them and their processes.

Hopefully, you will never confront this tragic event in your clients. The seemingly cosmic outrage that is a child's death is impossible to prepare for. As in other life events, however, your stance can make a difference in the lives of your clients and shade your relationships with greater depth and durability.

## Substance Abuse and Mental Illness

It is far from unusual to have substance abuse and mental health issues come across your desk as something being managed—or not—in your client families. A vast survey of a range of problems that can arise is well outside the purview of this book, never mind this chapter. But consistent with the message that managing wealth is profoundly about managing and developing "human capital" is the idea that there are some things even financial advisors can better understand so as to either be helpful or at a minimum do no harm.

### Substance Abuse

There are two base cases that bear some attention. The first is when, for example, the spouse of one of your direct clients let's slip that their husband or wife has a drinking or substance abuse problem that is getting out of hand. This is probably the least likely of scenarios but is not without precedent. In this case, you are in a direct advisor/client relationship and are being asked to at least take note of a problem if not actually do something about it. The second case—far more prevalent—is where you are dealing with a stakeholder who has a member of the family who is having difficulty. Often, this will come up because the person is a financial stakeholder as well, as in the case where the adolescent son or daughter of your client is the one having trouble.

In the first case, you have a couple of basic options, initially to pay attention to or ignore the situation that has been brought to your attention. In making this decision, you should review your own reactions in the context of asking the question of what is making them bring this up to you now. How are they viewing you such that it makes the surfacing of this topic with you possible? Is it a complaint being lodged with a trusted confidant? Is it an act of desperation on the part of a spouse who has lost boundary controls? How is the person about whom this declaration is made taking in what was said? Do they share in the belief that you were a proper audience for this revelation, and if so, what fantasies do they harbor about the role you might play in its resolution?

Normally, one would think this disclosure would hardly be the stuff of advisor-client discourse. Not so, when a good decade of effort has been spent among advisors to assume that golden position of "most trusted advisor."

This means that you have to be in a position not to do therapy but to assist in the management of the human side of wealth. Once you establish that the gesture of telling you about a mental health or substance abuse problem is a function of their trust for you—rather than an acting out with you as the latest audience—you can move into a more problem-solving mode. At the core of your ability to do anything will be the *desire to get help* on the part of the client. If this is not present, your odds of doing good are eclipsed by the greater likelihood that you will do harm by stepping into a familial conflict you are not contracted or trained to help solve. You will be dealing with partial and distorted information and will not be able to do even the most basic fact-finding. Your best bet at this juncture is to debrief the situation with a colleague and reapproach the couple about whether they would like a professional referral to sort through the complexities of the issues brought up. Ways you *can* help when there is a willingness to get help include:

- Clearly, sorting out any funding issues that might come with the new terrain.
- Develop a cadre of experts in your network who are knowledgeable about options for getting needed care, most frequently in the areas of couples and marital counseling, dual diagnosis, and substance abuse treatment.
- Develop a plan for the acquisition and consumption of needed services.
- Helping to sort out any issues bearing on competency or having implications for estate planning.

Just as you may not be the expert to execute a zero-cost collar, securitize an income stream or provide investment banking services to your client, so too in this case you are not the expert in the delivery of specialized services.

For many wealth advisors, however, you are in the role of orchestration and management of solutions, some of whom are going to be outside the traditional purview.

## Mental Illness

In your work, you will be unlikely to come across the major psychoses, particularly with adult clients. You will come across border conditions, or those minor to moderate conditions mental health workers call the "worried well." These individuals may exhibit depressive or manic processes, or obsessive-compulsive or borderline processes, and as we identified earlier, may make decisions where these pathologies are part of the mix in poor decision making. By and large, though, they will not be of the order of magnitude that warrants more than a careful referral to and follow up with a specialist.

In most cases regarding a more severe presentation will come through the second type of scenario described above where your direct client is trying to help someone else, often another family member. Classic among these situations is where a couple discloses to you that they have a child with escalating mental health or substance abuse problems.

To step back for a moment: Among the issues that should be coming through by now is what should become a rule of thumb for the new financial advisor, namely, that you should always be asking how members of the family are doing. And not just casually. As a key member of the advance guard of advisors helping families, you should always have a map of the family of your clients and tactfully inquire about *how they really are*. Most of the more severe issues, such as schizophrenia or substance abuse, are better identified early and intervened upon aggressively. If your clients respond to your inquiries by saying things like:

"Our son has never really had that many friends throughout junior high and high school."
"Jenny seems to really be struggling in school."
"We're worried about the kinds of friends that Robert has been hanging out with."
"Our daughter can't seem to concentrate."
"Philip can never seem to sit still, and it's starting to get in his way at school."

your job becomes to ask them to *tell you more*. Not because you will become a crack diagnostician. Nor because you'll know exactly what to do with the data you get. The fact is because of your new trusted role you may be the first person in their social system to pay attention to and pick up an emerging problem. Because many of the more serious problems emerging in adolescence and early adulthood evolve around learning disorders or attention-deficit/hyperactivity disorders (ADHD), early intervention can mean the difference between making some small but important adjustments to the kid's educational circumstances and the evolution of what are often "comorbid" syndromes and disorders that pile on the original problem, such as oppositional-defiant disorder (ODD), conduct disorder (CD) and poly–substance abuse disorders where children failed by the system around them begin to self-medicate using dangerous drugs.

Why do you care? Peter White, former Vice Chairman of Bank of America US Trust, framed the issue by saying that "When financial institutions do surveys of families, the top worry is always 'what about the children.' But they are never in a position to do anything about it."[3] This makes tremendous sense on one level. It is difficult to imagine in the most desirable world, for example, banks supplementing their core competencies by adding mental health services to the mix. Not a pretty image. And yet in the small moments and gestures, advisors can have and are having a tremendous impact by what Evan Roth, partner of the highly successful multifamily office BBR Partners, calls "having the courage to ask the next question, to go beyond the basic information clients provide," something Roth looks for as a core capability in their advisors.[4]

Identifying ADHD as a possible precursor to more serious development of comorbid conditions in the children of your clients is thus not to be confused with the real message: have the courage to ask the next question, to not be content with how everything is fine in Ward and June Cleaver's life. Often, the mere act of taking what your clients say seriously can prevent major derailments. You won't get paid for things that didn't happen. You will justify your wealth management fees by being explicit that you care enough about the "human capital" to inquire about its most basic circumstances and to help in the realization of its potential.

On a final note, it is also the case, as colleague Judith Stern Peck has described in her book on *Meaning and Money,* that no one has really written the book on parenting adult children. The joke is on all of us who believe that parenting stops with the "launch" of the child in their late teens and twenties. The facts of family life say otherwise, not the least so in the cases of family businesses, foundations, and family offices. Parents at 65 are often still worried about their forty-something children and are often faced with profound challenges in this forgotten land of hyperextended parenting. These children may be facing divorce, substance abuse and/or any of the transitions discussed here in their own children. It is important that the advisor be on the alert for these issues as well and not to be surprised at the immediacy of their presence in couples who should be simply "enjoying their final years now that the children are all grown up."

# Elder Care and End of Life Transitions

With never a dull moment in modern family life, at the other end of this hyperextended parenting fuse is the transition reversing parent and child roles in the final chapter of the elder generations' lives. We are here recalled to our own variant of the riddle of the Sphinx as articulated in Greek mythology. The base riddle, which Oedipus solves to spare his own life is:

> **Riddle**: What goes on four legs in the morning, on two legs at noon, and on three legs in the evening?
>
> **Solution**: A man, who crawls on all fours as a baby, walks on two legs as an adult, and walks with a cane in old age.

In our age, the cane can also represent the wealth in its broader, inclusive definition, on which the elders have to lean. In this broader symbolism, our interests go well beyond how the cane is financed. Often, the key developmental struggle for the family lies in how to answer which members make up the cane in the sense of how caregiving is balanced among family members and professional service providers. Invoking another metaphor, this "sandwich generation" is often compelled to rise to the occasion of parenting at least two generations, to figuring out how to do this among their siblings, and manage to take care of themselves in the process.[5]

## Siblings: Stepping Up and Getting Organized

Often "default" roles kick in among the siblings. Those who may live closer to Mom and Dad become conscripts in gradually increasing day-to-day maintenance roles. Those who live away probably did so for some reason whose logic now surfaces in the new context of not being there to pick up their share of the burden. As in many of the transitions we have discussed, this one may not bring out the best in sibling dynamics, though it has the potential to bring the siblings to a new level of collaborative functioning as well.

Of course, the "elephant in the living room" invariably has to do with the degradation of functioning in one or more parents, that parent's potential reaction and that of the spouse. The range of tools, such as those associated with testamentary planning, medical directives, and financial scenario modeling continue to have their place in support of desired family outcomes. Additionally critical is the on-ramp that is built to enable the family to approach their parents with difficult decisions, as when discussions of the need for increased levels of care or estate plans loom large.

## Difficult Conversations

The preparation for a series of family meetings can be among the most important services advisors can provide in this context. More often than not, you will be working with a family that has any number of the following resistances to having these kinds of meetings:

- "If I bring up estate planning issues, I will be perceived as being overly interested in the money."
- "My brother will balk if I ask him for help with Mom and Dad."
- "We live too far away and are too busy to get this done."
- "My parents will be insulted."
- "My parents will be hurt."
- "My parents will be outraged."
- "Why should I expect my siblings to be helpful now? They haven't helped out for years."
- "If I keep this up by myself, my sibs will nominate me for sainthood."
- "If I keep this up by myself, I can continue to use martyrdom and guilt to get other things I want."
- "If we talk about estate planning, we might bring on our parents' death."
- "If I don't think about this, it will all go away."

The advisor usually is working in a force field where these and other resistances are occurring in different members of the family, only one or two of which is usually a direct client. This means that the advisor's efficacy in this situation will occur first around his or her ability to keep their eye on the need for the family to meet, to educate their client(s) on possible sources of resistance, and to help their immediate clients identify both their own resistances and fears. As a map of this force field emerges, a strategy can be developed to inch the family toward the series of meetings that is believed to be needed. Notice, too, that I have used meetings in the plural to reflect that this transition is not likely to be buttoned up in a single encounter, but will instead require a series of meetings. Keeping what we've discussed in mind about family meetings, thought should be given to the type of meeting needed and whether, for example, some might even be better managed through conference calls.

As in other transitions, the concept of time will be playing out differently for different family participants. For one, the need for someone to talk to Dad about surrendering his driver's license may be palpably urgent. For another, some transparency in an otherwise opaque estate plan may be equally urgent. More important still may be the need to process the scary eventualities embedded in this kind of transition. As in other transitions, great care should be taken to not let *transactions* dominate the *transitions* that need to be made. If the first face-to-face meeting, once it occurs, is simply dominated by attention to the "fact pattern" of the matter and none to the emotional processing that is being set in motion, the risk that an effective transition will not take place will rise. In some cases, having a meeting about *why we don't want to be having THIS meeting* can be a better place to start than jumping, for example, right into a big confrontation of Mom or Dad about how they need to move into assisted living or remove Dad from life support as soon as possible.

There is no formula for how this should unfold. One thing the advisor can trust, however, is that if he or she listens to and stays steady with what outcomes are sought and what resistances may be in play, the family knows on some level what it is facing and what it must do. This knowledge is resident in the family system. Your job is to help whatever family members you have in front of you tease this out and make sure that they are attending to both kinds of timing (clock time and psychological time) that need to be honored in the process. Doing this will help ensure that your interventions serve in some large or small way to enable the transition under way rather than handicap it.

---

## Tips and Takeaways for the New Financial Advisor

We have moved in this chapter at light speed through a limited set of major life events and transitions. Without having a prayer of being exhaustive, we nevertheless have some conclusions that can be drawn. What is common about these life transitions is that the new financial advisor has in each instance an embedded opportunity to honorably side with change in the system that is in part under his or her care. As we've understood from earlier chapters, this capability largely lies in the advisor's ability to listen both to him- or herself and to the client system through the representatives is has offered as formal clients. It also lies in decisions about what to pay explicit attention to in client dialogues and what to ignore. In each case, as a trusted agent in the lives of the families you can choose to hear more than you would be expected to and as a result to enhance your utility to the system rather than slip into irrelevance, or worse, into a source of stasis when it is change that is needed.

We also know that role and identity changes are at the core of what is going on, not only changes in estate planning needs or asset allocations. We know these changes in role and identity can have positive or negative sequelae. As financial advisors, we have limits in our ability to positively change things and we should not overstate our power in these situations. But make no mistake that our families are consciously or not asking for more, for integrated advice and counsel at the various flashpoints of wealth and family life. More and more, we have a front-row seat in life's interactive theater and are being asked to be participant-observers, if not core players in the important dramas before us. This opportunity is ours to squander.

# CHAPTER 7

# Enabling Advisors

## *Open Letter to a Financial Institution about What the New Financial Advisor Needs to Succeed*

You now have a number of tools and ideas in hand as a new financial advisor. You know that to provide services in this evolving market, you have to better understand yourself (since you are by far the most valuable tool), understand the psychological and familial terrain in which your clients operate, deliver a different range of services (and get paid for them), and develop new ways of assisting clients in meeting a range of life challenges (or at least do no harm in the process). You are now in a position to more genuinely practice the emerging discipline of family wealth management, with all this means regarding the familial as well as financial dimensions of the work.

The next challenge arises because you are not doing this work in a vacuum. Whether you are an independent registered investment advisor or insurance professional, or a captive provider, you do need to pay attention to the enabling (or disabling) environment in which you are delivering these services. We deliver these services in a force field, where some forces serve to support changes we are making and some serve to stifle them. That is the reality of the situation.

As a financial advisor, you know that you need help delivering this service because you do not have the hours in the day to profitably or productively deliver it by yourself. Some of you work in financial institutions as a means to facilitate service delivery. Others work in a continuum of small to medium-size businesses and outsource some of the core services, such as asset custody, brokerage, underwriting, and financial product implementation. Wherever you are situated, your institutional or platform sponsors are in at least two businesses: enabling you and profiting from you. No need to get sentimental about it. Relationships with your employer often have a

Faustian quality, with hostage taking not unusual on both sides. It's sometimes an uneasy alliance with all varieties of push and pull affecting service
delivery to clients. Add new role pressures we are discussing here and you
have the makings of yet more strife between you and your sponsor. So if it
weren't difficult enough, you are now also in the business of helping your
platform provider change? Cheer up. There is some good news with regard
to ways sponsors and platform providers are changing to better enable advisory work. And, to a greater or lesser extent, they do listen to advisory
leaders—which you are on the way to becoming.

This chapter is meant to speak to contextual complexities associated
with changing the way advisory businesses are able to transform themselves
into solution-centric businesses that have the realization of life outcomes in
clients as their reason for being.

The core of this chapter is presented through the means of an open letter
to the chief executive of the financial institution (or platform provider). It
is meant to be suggestive of the kind of dilemmas and dialogues that are
occurring and should occur as the industry shifts away from being product-
centric to solution-centric in the delivery of services to clients and their
families. For the purposes of informing you how to organize your proposal,
I have inserted headings throughout the letter; however, when reading these
different sections please keep in mind that each part is a continuation of
the letter that I suggest you compose. After the letter concludes, I end the
chapter with Tips and Takeaways for the New Financial Advisor.

## To Whom This May Concern

*Imagine, then, that you are in the shoes of the advisor below, who is writ-
ing this to his chief executive. Your personal letter might be different—and
I would encourage you as you read what follows to imagine what you
might add or take away. In the end, it is meant to stimulate thought
and dialogue beyond just you and your client and on to the institutions
and service providers that enable you to reach your potential as a new
financial advisor.*

Dear Chief Executive of My Financial Institution:

I am writing this letter to you and copying my manager in hopes of
gaining help with some challenges I am having in my daily work for this
firm. I have been thinking about things that were said at our last major
offsite about where the industry and our company are going. [I was
pleased you were able to attend, because I know that you have well
more than the wealth management side of the company to manage.]

I am also taking seriously the proposed idea that even though I am not among the senior most advisors in the firm that my input is encouraged and welcome.

## Who I Am and What I Am Seeing

First I should tell you about my background. I started in this business as a broker and did very well. Not too many years ago I also became a financial planner, and more recently have embraced our fee-based business model that has begun to predominate in the industry. By and large, I have kept up with industry changes and have been quite successful in my career. While I have been at this firm only a few years, I am hopeful that this is a place I can work for many years to come.

The other day I was with one of my wealthier clients and his wife. They had recently attended the seminar we have been running around the country for clients on "affluenza and raising financially responsible children." I did not have the occasion to attend this seminar, but I have read a few articles on the topic in the *Journal* and on the Internet. Over the years, I have also seen my share of clients with bratty, entitled children, but only recently have I begun to see it a lot. I often feel sorry for some of these parents, who have worked so hard to get what they have only to have their kids turn out this way.

In any case, my clients were in my office the other day and said how much they appreciated the seminar. They said it made them feel less alone in what they face with their children. They also saw the company they keep with these issues; they were impressed with the other clients in the room and did not feel as "crazy" as a result. They told me they did not feel quite so bad as parents or like they were as big a failure as they thought they were in their own minds.

But then it got more interesting. And, to be candid, for me more uncomfortable. They said they wanted to follow up with what was said in the session. They said their motivation to learn and make changes that they felt could help their children better know "the value of a dollar" was high and that they wanted to make a priority of changing things for their kids. They explained some of what is happening with their 17- and 14-year-olds, and why they were worried. I had heard some of this before but hadn't paid it much mind. Then they turned to *me*. They asked me what they should do. They said that our firm clearly knew what they were talking about and that they have built great trust in me and that they wanted to follow up in specific ways that would work for their family. Candidly, I felt completely on the spot and taken off guard. I knew the seminar was intended to educate clients—I did not know

(*Continued*)

would then have to respond intelligently to what now seems like a legitimate request. We raised the issue, and they wanted to follow up!

## I Am Not Prepared for This

Now, I am pretty good on my feet. You have to be to be as successful in this business as I have been. But I will tell you that this was one of the more uncomfortable moments in my career—and believe me I've been through a number of interesting moments in my work with high-net-worth clients. I did in this case manage to stumble through a few recommendations—you know, do an allowance, save some, give some to charity, that type of thing. But I was out on a limb. I responded but my response was canned, and I didn't even much believe it myself. They were grateful for my suggestions, but I could tell that they fell flat, and that is something I am not used to doing to clients.

I thought of referring them to a counselor or a therapist, but I didn't feel comfortable doing this because I didn't think they were "sick" that way. What I did know is that they would take it badly if I even suggested therapy. Moreover, I didn't really know whom I would refer them to because it seems that the issues they are having *do have to do with money.* I don't know what a therapist would do with this issue even if they got the referral.

I have been in the business long enough to know that we no longer retain clients based on investment returns. If that were true, there would be much more turnover in assets than actually happens. Clients stay because of the relationships we establish with them and the problems we help them solve.

So I felt for the first time out of my depth. I truly didn't know what to do with these clients. On top of that, I started to imagine that these would not be the last clients to darken my doorway with these types of concerns.

## Where Do I Go for Help?

This prompted me to take the step of calling the expert who ran our seminar to ask for guidance. She was very nice and gave me a number of tips I could give this couple in particular, but she said that she could not continue to have these conversations unless further business arrangements between her and the firm could be made to do this work.

I also talked to a couple of guys I trust in the wealth management group and they were supportive, too, but didn't really add to the "tip" list I had already gotten from the seminar leader.

This started eating at me to the point that I started thinking *I* was nuts. What was I thinking? I'm their financial advisor, not their shrink.

Moreover, I started imagining a talk with my manager about this (and then actually had one). Initially, I couldn't even figure out how to frame the problem. First of all, I tried to put myself in his shoes. He is a very successful manager of producers and has been very good over the years in getting his team to increase asset balances over and over. His approach as long as I've known him has been to help us remove any and all barriers to gathering assets—and he's darn good at it, among the best I've worked for. He has also been good at helping us keep the assets we've gathered, though I would say he's better at the former than the latter. [He knows this, too. I'm not speaking out of school here.] In fairness, too, he is better compensated on net new assets anyway, so that is naturally his focus day in and day out.

So here I am imagining this talk and realizing that I don't really know how to put it together or what I might really be asking for. Would he come up with a multistep program for working with this client couple? Where would he have gotten something like this? Why would he even care? Would I simply be transferring to him the strange situation I am in without setting the stage for him to successfully advise me? And given our quarterly targets and annual hunt, how much time could either one of us spend on figuring this out, especially since we already manage north of three quarters of the assets this family has?

## Beyond Stirring Up the Market

Then I was forced to think further about whose problem this really was. The family's problem, of course. And mine to the extent that I had given them only a lukewarm solution, more like a tiny bandage on a growing wound vulnerable to a festering familial infection. I also remembered something Jay Hughes said when he came to our firm about how failure in families was the rule not the exception.

Then, quite candidly, I started to think about the firm's responsibility.

Please hear me out. I don't mean anything wrong by this great institution.

Our firm did sow these seeds with my client. Somebody knew something. We don't just offer up seminars to our clients for nothing. Because the budget for this event came out of marketing, someone over there knew something about this. (I did place a call over to marketing and they said that in fact there were several surveys done in 2005 and 2006 at our firm and in the industry that lent strong support to the idea that among the most important things on high-net-worth clients'

*(Continued)*

minds is how their children, young and young adult, are faring.) When I probed a bit more about how we should follow up, I was mostly told about how to generate new meetings and update the CRM.

When they said this about the CRM, it actually made me think further about the tools I might need to follow up with this couple. I know that because we are only one of three major businesses (commercial, retail, and wealth management), we inherit tools and technologies that are not always about us. We don't really hold much sway when it comes to significant technology investments, and I understand this. When I really tried to list out what I might need to work with this couple, though, I was hard pressed to know how I would support the project work that might need to be done and what kinds of metrics I would be tracking to know if what I was doing was working. How would I help the family do the discovery that might need to take place in order to properly frame the problem? What assessment tools might I use to help in this process and how would I ever get trained to use them properly? Not to be a complainer, but I don't even like the financial modeling tools we have and often have to build my own spreadsheets to work with clients around content I'm familiar with! They only seem to crunch numbers directionally toward products we are selling—which is fine, too. Again, don't misunderstand me.

## How Do We Get Paid—or *Our* Issues with Money

I figured from here that it would be a good thing to actually charge for services I was expecting to render. Then I really hit a wall. Not only did I not know how to price what I might do, but I did not really even know who I would ask to help me figure this out. This turned out to be a multilayered problem, since at the start, I don't even usually talk that much about pricing to clients beyond the fee breakpoints. I don't really handle money at all and only know at a basic level that in the asset-gathering business, clients these days are difficult to gain and easy to lose—just when they actually start to get really profitable. I wouldn't really know how to make a proposal to do work that wasn't along the standard lines for investments, and I wouldn't know how to value my time in doing this work other than through a crude calculation of what my hourly or per diem rates might be on a cost-plus basis.

Further, I couldn't imagine going to my manager to solicit his help. Again, he is great and at the top of his game. I just think the game itself has changed right before our eyes, and it was amusing to imagine going to him with a plan to do a project with a client that needed to be proposed, priced, and sold on a completely different basis.

I also began to get embarrassed at the angst I was developing about all this. After all, pretty much everything we do for clients to get them and keep them is already being paid for! The beauty of charging 85 to 95 basis points for assets under management, of course, is that it is automatically deducted, is recurring, and has enough margin to subsidize our other services. This meant that I could go back to this couple, do a (hopefully) small project for them, and not have to ask for compensation. What was my problem, after all?

I should have taken comfort in the fact that we have been training clients for years to expect this one fee that we will sneak out of their funds in such a way as to almost not be noticed. And wow, before March 2000 these fees were handsome indeed! Still, I could not slip this nagging feeling that there was something wrong or that we had backed ourselves into a corner. I kept thinking about the delta between the pricing of our products and the value we were attempting to create. I wondered several ways about whether that single fee was a luxury or a noose around our necks and whether our affair with asset-based fees hadn't in fact backed us into a corner.

I remembered the previous firm I worked for where we gave away estate and financial planning in the 90s at certain asset levels and fired all of those who delivered these services in the first quarter of 2001, apparently because we could no longer subsidize their existence with asset-based fees.

I also tried to again imagine what I would say to my clients if I were to charge them for the discovery services I had concocted to help them work through a solution with their children. I had to laugh at myself, you know, an anxious laugh, because I didn't have the first clue as to what I would say. Just imagining this conversation ran my anxiety through the roof. You see, I'm no more comfortable talking about money than my clients are. I like the fact that my discourse with clients is confined to performance conversations and only rarely about fees.

## Empathy for Management

In fact, I really don't know why I am raising all this. It actually seems to only be pregnant with issues I don't know how to approach on my own. Nor do I seem able to locate a resource in the firm—other than yourself—to share this with or get good advice.

Even as I say that, I imagine I put you in a peculiar position. So I tried to imagine the situation you're in opposite some of what I'm saying.

First of all, you are running a large publicly traded company and thus serve at the pleasure of the board, who in turn have analyst and

*(Continued)*

shareholder expectations to manage. You also have your three major unit heads to manage as well as the other C-level officers. In this context, you expect your wealth management head to deliver steady return growth that reflects profitable revenue enhancement that meets or exceeds peer production. I also know that, because you did not come from the investment side of the business, you're not likely to want to drill too deep on how this unit-level contribution is derived. And how could you possibly do so with all the responsibilities you carry. (Lots of hubris on my part that you might even read this!)

So let me be clear. I have lots of empathy for you and your task. Shareholders, for one, do not see things across the time horizons that we are discussing in this letter. They send you mixed messages to manage: some of their capital is "patient" and hopes that you will continue to take steps that, while difficult in the short run, actually anticipate change and build future value. Others act like fussy day traders wringing their hands at the slightest hint of share stagnation or depression. They have short fuses and may even call for your head.

They also have extreme dislike for anything that smacks of consulting or project revenue in our industry. While we know that other industries have weathered the shift from product-centric to solution-centric models (think IBM or, say, SunGard) and have done extremely well, this concept is well out of the canon in our field. You would risk heresy to say that in 5 to 7 years as much as 40 percent to 50 percent of wealth management revenue would come from consulting revenue, just as it happened in key technology businesses. And it would not only be outside stakeholders who would think you'd lost a screw.

So even if you did think there was merit in supporting the kinds of projects I was contemplating with my clients and their kids, to announce such a reform would probably render the wealth management unit one large deer in the headlights. It's not hard to imagine the chaos:

- "I wasn't trained for this!"
- "How will I get paid?"
- "We have no systems!"
- "Our clients will balk at all the new fees!"
- "I'm leaving and going to a competitor!"

The position you would be put in, far from being enviable, would have everyone at your heels, including the other unit heads, whose first thought would be that they were going to be net investors in this strange and dangerous endeavor. They would likely feel that they would bear the earnings brunt of this strange voyage.

## Conflicting Cultures

I remember Jay Hughes saying that financial institutions have to manage both quantitative and qualitative cultures, and that these are far from compatible. I know that when some advisors have gone out to do this business independently, at least one advantage they seem to feel they have is the opportunity to build a company that is not capitalized with public money so they do not have the headaches someone in your position has. It also enables them to deploy more patient capital at the challenge in front of us. I'm just a small player, but I think they may have a point. They may have bought the kind of time it takes to reinvent the business in a more solution-centric mode.

But I don't think we should resign ourselves too easily to the intractability of our dilemmas. Furthermore, I was always taught that you don't bring a boss a problem unless you also are bringing a solution.

So I further tried to put myself in your shoes. I have thought that part of the way one might think about this is in evolutionary rather than revolutionary terms. The difference is partly one of velocity: revolutionary action is accelerated and violent; in many cases the blowback after the event is as bad or worse, leaving employee populations surrounded with casualties and feet dug in. Evolutionary change is gradual and based on diversity. Different approaches are seeded, cultivated, and either die off or pick up their own momentum. Revolution connotes a stark before and after. Evolution says a new, more fit species often comes from *difference*.

## What We Can Do

I know that I am not the only one in our firm who is intrigued by the kinds of issues that our clients are bringing up. One of the reasons I did not attend the seminar the other day was that its organizers didn't want to have more advisors in the room than clients. This means that there is more than a little nascent interest in the advisor base about these kinds of challenges. We should find a way to capitalize on this drive and begin to source the individuals in the firm that could be part of this evolution toward a business that has as its objective the facilitation of family wealth management in all its familial *and* financial meanings.

The next step might be to set up a pilot project to generate a "proof of concept" on which further strategies might be developed. I think this pilot could have some of the following components:

- You and our unit head could act as sponsors for the pilot, sending the signal that an experimental space was going to be created in
  *(Continued)*

which new business models were going to be tested for the next couple of years.

- An interunit advisory committee is inaugurated to provide supervision and management of the pilot project.
- The unit recruits an interdisciplinary team to carry out the pilot. These team members:
  - Are not paid directly for asset balances.
  - Place similar proportions of compensation as base and "at risk" as in their existing jobs, with a reasonable possibility of meeting their past-year compensation numbers.
  - Are strongly motivated to participate in ways not only measurable in financial terms.
  - Receive stock options to further tie in their interests with shareholders.
  - Are given a budget within which to acquire things like training and tools.
- A select set of clients and prospects are recruited over time to join in this experiment. Their reactions and experiences will provide a compass for how services are priced and delivered.

Overall, this pilot would serve to generate learning for the organization in a risk-managed environment. Flying somewhat below the radar, this project could be expected to:

- Train advisors to build new practices into day-to-day routines.
- Test new business models.
- Drive tools, technologies, and reporting toward the new realities of alternative service delivery mechanisms supporting the new business.

What this might help us mitigate are some of the following risks we might have taken, including:

- Telling the market we are about delivering against life outcomes and give advisors nothing in support of this value proposition.
- Fund all of our family-related programming out of marketing budgets, thus extending the idea that this programming is simply meant to generate sales and not really have an impact beyond that.
- Overinvest in shotgun, stand-up training that may not help advisors day to day with this new role.
- Pay only on asset balances and leave ourselves without a "next chapter" in the evolution of our business.

- Take too big a step, knowing that if culture change is at stake, it needs to be measured in years, not quarters.

These are some ideas I have been working on in light of changes I am sensing in the mutual expectations being set—and not always delivered on—between us and our clients. I am hopeful we can sustain a dialogue in support of the changes we need to implement in order to remain competitive and serve the evolving mission we have in relation to our clients.
    Sincerely,
    Senior Client Advisor

## Tips and Takeaways for the New Financial Advisor

We have explored the nature of changes taking place in the world of the new financial advisor. We started with the person of the advisor and the psychology and dynamics of clients around money and how this can unfold during transitions. We have discussed service model changes and the use of family meetings and other interventions that can enhance your effectiveness with clients. All along, I have stressed the need to do this with the input of others. The role changes increasingly demanded of the new financial advisor are too big to take on in isolation.

This chapter says that the other key constituencies needed for this shift include management and platform providers. The dialogue needed may not sound exactly like our senior advisor's appeal to the CEO of his financial institution, but it needs to be enlivened in such a way as to affect the day-to-day practice of family wealth management and not just the occasional events staged for clients. The message for the new financial advisor is to not be passive in how this dialogue takes shape. Many top executives in the family wealth management business know well what is changing. The reports have been coming in now for several years about the commoditization of the business and the need to differentiate on service. The directions are clear, but the mechanisms of change remain elusive. The new financial advisor—those at the sharp edge of working with clients—should give voice wherever possible to what is needed to support the real changes that now need to be made in the business of family wealth management. Because you are the closest to these changes, your voice needs to be heard at all levels of the industry.

# CHAPTER 8

# Skill Development for Your New Role

I mproving your skill set for the new environment no doubt seems daunting. The universe of continuing education is still sparse with offerings that support you in developing the skills you need to integrate financial data and family data into your service delivery system. And while training can be useful, there is no substitute in my view for finding ways to change the way you work day in and day out. We previously looked at how you can change your service model to incorporate new intervention methods into all client interactions. We also argued that you are the key instrument that needs to be refined. We now turn to skill development protocols that can help you build competency and confidence in how you face off against the important work of changing lives.

This chapter is organized by two themes: assessment and development. The first involves helping you through a structured self-assessment process using a simple 360-degree model where you rate yourself along several competencies and, where possible, have staff, colleagues, and/or clients rate you along these competencies as well. (For your reference, I will list these competencies in an organized assessment worksheet.)

The logic of this is straightforward. I may think I'm a good listener, but if I ask everyone from my kids to my colleagues to rate me, I may find a different perspective altogether. When I find differences from my own self-perception, I can either ignore this information or actually probe its significance. The best way to do the latter is usually to not simply take a lower rating at face value but to invite someone to describe a critical incident during which they felt I was not listening. This conversation is where the value begins to accrue, because it begins to help me understand the specific kinds of circumstances where I have lapses in listening and whether there are patterns to be alert to in how these lapses emerge.

The second theme provides you with the means to create a realistic and practical development plan that enables you to make progress over an extended period of time. There is no one way to do this. This chapter is meant to provide a supportive structure in which to enhance your ability to work more effectively at that unique juncture of wealth and family life. For most, this kind of learning will need to be bite-size and practical. We will also revisit the peer-supervisory model, which is adapted to this environment from supervision models designed to train psychiatrists and psychologists. Remember, this journey is one that is best taken with others. This is a message that will be reinforced throughout this chapter. Not only is it more difficult to do this alone, it is many times less effective.

In this chapter, I will discuss three basic approaches that financial advisors may take in assessing and developing their skill set. Using the framework for skill assessment provided, I then define the various skills that the new financial advisor must possess and discuss how they effectively generate positive life outcomes for your clients.

# The Approach to Skill Development

An important assumption I am making in this chapter is that you have full mastery of one of the core disciplines of wealth management. These are typically the disciplines of investments, law, risk management, and taxation. The skills described here are meant to augment your existing skill set in a way that is directionally in the service of improving your work with families. These skill areas are also not exhaustive in depth, and I believe that most advisors can expect to excel deeply in only one or two disciplines through their career.

## The Emerging "Languages" of Family Wealth Management

In talking about the general knowledge base that new financial advisors must have, I have found a powerful analogy in language training and in the larger notion of analysis of discourses. To a large extent, the new financial advisor is, quite literally, speaking a new language. In learning a new language, one hopefully proceeds through the following progression:

- *Conversational.* At this level, I am able to have simple conversations that enable me to get around in another language. I can order dinner, find a restroom, give directions to a cab driver, and ask for help.
- *Fluent.* This next level means I can actually carry on a conversation of more than a few sentences. I can spend the evening navigating a party in another language.

- *Literate.* Not only am I able at this level to speak the language, but I can also read it. I can also write it in the sense of being able to fill out forms and correspond in the language.
- *Authorship.* At this highest level, I can do all of the previous activities but am also able to write at the level of publishable discourse. By this time, I know the language nearly as well as a native speaker, and in some cases even better.

Because wealth management is postdisciplinary—that is, it represents for the current generation of advisors a new discipline that incorporates and supersedes the previous disciplines that make it up—the "languages" are virtually impossible to completely master. Nor is it necessary, in my view, to master them all. The industry would come to a halt if this were the case. These various languages—of taxes, risk management, investments, business, finance, psychology, real estate, and philanthropy—can be looked at in this way: the new financial advisor should strive for literacy and/or authorship levels of understanding and competence in a core discipline, as well as strive to become at least conversational in the ancillary disciplines. In this model, I have seen advisors in law become fluent and even literate in the discourse of family dynamics, but on a broad level, it is perfectly sufficient in my mind that the attainment of the conversational level is reached, if only because it is as steep a hill to climb as it would be for a psychologist to develop deep knowledge of all manner of investments. In addition, becoming conversational means that you know enough to know what you don't know and to ask for help when you need it. As you proceed through this chapter, keep in mind that, just as in learning a new language, you will need to assess yourself, clarify your weaker areas, and create the circumstances in which you can practice what you are learning.

## A Note on Setting SMART Objectives for Yourself

The process of learning this "new language" should begin, however, by taking a realistic look at what is possible to do in the interstices of your everyday busy life. The work of the new financial advisor represents a steep hill to climb, and it is important that you set goals and objectives for yourself that are achievable in light of the circumstances in which you find yourself, and don't leave you feeling frustrated at how everything from your revenue mix to your service model is not changing at the speed you'd like.

Thus, when it comes to setting developing objectives for yourself, it does not hurt to use SMART processes to screen them:

- **S**pecific: who, what, when, where, which and why.
- **M**easurable: how much, how many, how will I know.

- **A**ttainable: expand your horizons but not to the extent of creating yet another obstacle.
- **R**ealistic: you are both willing and able to reach the goal.
- **T**imely: what time frame is needed and is this the right time?

These kinds of objectives can sustain your motivation to make progress and keep you from getting overwhelmed and discouraged. It is also extremely useful, as if you haven't heard this from me before, to vet your objectives with trusted colleagues—do not do this alone, as it will be extremely difficult to sustain.

## Hughes's *Personne d'affaires* and *Personne de Confiance*

We also need to take a moment to differentiate the notion of skills from those of qualities that are needed to do this work. While there is always some overlap, skills or competencies tilt in the direction of what you can *do* and qualities toward who you need to *be*. In the latter case, advisors should consult the work of Jay Hughes, who elegantly articulates qualities that can be found in great advisors.[1] These qualities are set in the context of Hughes's differentiation between the advisor who is the *personne d'affaires* and the one who elects—and is elected by key families—to become the *personne de confiance*.

To sharpen this distinction, the *personne d'affaires* is one who is highly skilled in the purveyance of goods and services. In our world, this might represent a skilled estate attorney, financial planner, or investment advisor.

> [Personnes d'affaires are] *generally persons providing families with financial products, goods, and services, which the family needs for the dynamic stewardship and conservation of its financial capital. Generally, they are not in the business of seeking to grow the family's human and intellectual capital, nor are they personally energized by the family.[2]*

By contrast, the *personne de confiance* connotes consigliore or the family's most trusted counsel. They are all but one of the family and serve as the most trusted counselor on virtually all matters of family well-being and strategy. Again to quote from Hughes:

> *Once they've had success in serving the family's financial needs, some* personnes d'affaires *begin to experience a strong conviction that they could be of more services to the family if they could help with the growth of its human and intellectual capital. . . . Often these feelings result from a particular family asking questions of them that go beyond the products and services they've become expert at providing. . . . They seek a different way of being a serving professional.[3]*

Among the characteristics of this latter class of advisor is a set of aspirational standards we should all aspire to, and include:

- An interest in the art of governance.
- A belief in orderly evolutionary change.
- Skepticism without contempt.
- Subordination of ambition to a higher calling.

In this chapter, by contrast, we are looking more closely at skill sets that support the "blocking and tackling" that, in combination with the right characteristics, lead to advisor greatness. Another way to put it is that these skills are necessary but insufficient by themselves to drive greatness. These skills should, however, add to your baseline skills, whether you are in the role of *personne d'affaires* or *personne de confiance*. These skills are summarized in Table 8.1 and are examined in more detail below. Regardless of whether you aspire to the role of personne d'affaires or personne de confiance, the skills we examine below form the basis of the effective delivery of advice in the world of the new financial advisor, regardless of the underlying vocational model you choose in the end.

Table 8.1 can also act as a worksheet for you to do your own self-assessment of your skill levels but also to give to others around you, such as colleagues, clients, and subordinates, to see how synchronized your self-reporting is with those who know you. The most valid 360-degree ratings of this kind are given by individuals who have known you for 1 to 3 years. There is also room to identify your priority areas for development and to indicate who in your universe can be conscripted to help you design an action plan.

We can now turn to each skill area listed in Table 8.1 to define them in more detail.

## Communication

Everyone knows they need the basics of communication to be an effective advisor. To lean into this work you need to take these basics in additional directions to sharpen your ability to work with complex financial families. Deep listening, empathy, the ability to deliver difficult or controversial information, and special reporting and presentation skills form the next level of competencies to operate with family clients.

### Deep Listening

Many advisors are not good listeners in the sense it is given here. The kind of listening advocated here is not sales-oriented listening, which has its place. I

TABLE 8.1    Framework for Skills Assessment

| Capability | Skill Level | | | |
|---|---|---|---|---|
| | **Poor** | **Fair** | **Good** | **Excellent** |
| **Communication** | | | | |
| Listens deeply to others, labels affect and process dynamics, provides basic feedback, effectively uses silence | | | | |
| Develops and conveys empathy for clients | | | | |
| Delivers difficult and potentially controversial messages in a constructive manner | | | | |
| Constructs financial and familial reports/presentations that are consumable by clients with different learning styles | | | | |
| **Comfort in Talking about Money** | | | | |
| Ability to talk about highly charged money matters | | | | |
| Discusses and asks for fair compensation for services; collaboratively helps families place a value on services | | | | |
| Timing: sequences and paces conversational topics for when they are most likely to be heard | | | | |
| **Family Systems** | | | | |
| Assesses the strengths and vulnerabilities of families | | | | |
| Ability to work with a subset of family members while keeping the whole system in mind | | | | |
| Determines optimal involvement levels for various system participants (family/nonfamily) to realize objectives | | | | |
| Intervenes in ways that promote positive conflict resolution in client systems | | | | |
| **Collaboration and Leadership** | | | | |
| Assesses and forms constructive alliances with the family's advisory system | | | | |
| When required, leads teams of advisors toward effective results for clients | | | | |
| When required, follows the leadership of other advisors; is a good team member | | | | |
| Sources and effectively integrates experts with the wealth team | | | | |

TABLE 8.1   (*Continued*)

| Capability | Skill Level | | | |
| --- | --- | --- | --- | --- |
| | Poor | Fair | Good | Excellent |
| **Integration** | | | | |
| Effectively analyzes human and financial data to determine their relative constibutions to client challenges | | | | |
| Intervenes to privilege family well-being over financial well-being where there is the potential for conflict | | | | |
| Creatively deploys financial strategies as interventions affecting life outcomes | | | | |

| Prioritization (rank those areas that need the most attention first) | Who will help you design an action plan? |
| --- | --- |
| 1. _____ | 1. _____ |
| 2. _____ | 2. _____ |
| 3. _____ | 3. _____ |
| 4. _____ | 4. _____ |

have listened to advisors in sales mode who are great at listening for product feature and benefits hooks in their clients. By contrast, deep listening is among the most powerful skills you can develop and is marked by your ability to hear into the desires being expressed by clients together with the defenses, ambivalences, and impediments that surround these desires.

This kind of listening is driven out of a genuine curiosity about what makes the other tick. It is very data driven in the sense that it pays close attention to the speech and discourse of the other, to the voice of the speaker (role), its relationship to what is being said (passive, active, ambivalent) and the others not present whose voices mingle with what is being said (echoes of Mom, Dad, siblings, other advisors). This kind of listening is disciplined and scientific in its appraisal of what is being heard; it provides data that can be relied on in the formulation of hypotheses that can be tested. This listener clears a space and focuses attention on the client in a way that is unmistakable from one who is merely listening for an angle through which to insert him- or herself or product discourse.

The deep listener differentiates between productive and unproductive silences, and knows in the former that these are "working silences." Things are getting done. Sometimes these are difficult silences, and what most needs to be managed is the advisor's training to always look the expert—which means filling the air with pressured speech about what one knows. There is a time and a place to let one's expert discourse reign; deep listening wisdom helps you know when this should happen and when it's time to shut up and allow the silence to work its magic with the client.

## Empathy

Empathy is a simple idea that is difficult to execute, especially in circumstances in which the advisor's wealth is but a rounding error of the client's. It refers to the simplicity of standing in someone else's shoes, to live in their skin. One can debate the metaphysical possibility of doing this, but one cannot deny that the effects of empathic processes are palpable. It may be hard to imagine that clients as wealthy as yours have experienced anything near what those of us in the "great unwashed" experience. And indeed, the blinding manufacture of barriers between the haves and have-nots can at least in part be described as a massive empathic failure. The message here becomes this: don't be distracted about the question as to whether you can actually step into another's shoes; at bottom, it is the sustained attempt to do so that matters. Clients will know when you show empathy. You will know when you are trying to be empathic, and it is the trying that matters. Whether you will ever know what it's like to step into your own private jet matters less than the attempt to hear the jet owner's regret that he bought a jet—with all the attendant and unanticipated headaches involved—instead of acquiring the same services through a fractional share program.

Empathy takes practice for many, and its effects accumulate. It will help you in every way lay the groundwork for effective responses when you hear about the drug addictions, divorces, and deaths that will present themselves to you through your clients. It will make you a bigger person and a candidate for the role of the *personne de confiance*. It will make you a new financial advisor.

## Delivering Difficult and Controversial Messages

Bringing difficult news: Hardly something anyone wants to do. But what we are talking about is what in some circles is akin to "speaking truth to power." This means that you have built the skills to package your most difficult messages in ways that invite the best possible reception by your client. It might, for example, mean having the courage to say to a client that if he does not also set up a (smaller) trust for his daughter-in-law, that should she and his son divorce, he runs the risk that a certain trajectory of resentment of him may build up in his grandchildren. Or it might mean saying that the contemplated estate plan will surely save taxes but also looks like a veritable blueprint for generations of family misery.

Peter White has characterized this problem by saying that many advisors have gotten caught up in the retail business adage that "the customer is always right." This has often rendered the advisor more like someone just taking orders, however ridiculous, outrageous, or destructive they are. He describes this as a vicious circle in which people treat the wealthy with undue deference, which then invites them to assume ever greater amounts of deference in their service providers. This in turn promotes a certain kind of entitlement, which mushrooms into the production of virtually spoiled individuals whose every whim must be served. In the end, this generates a pact of censorship in which the advisor is rendered more and more silent with respect to the delivery of messages that may have strategic import for the overall management of wealth but may not be easy to take in by the client system. It is hard to train the courage element in this, but it is not hard to get better at packaging these kinds of messages in ways that are diplomatic, clear, and consumable by your audience.

## Reports and Presentations

Reporting and presentation constructs in the industry are profoundly supply side in orientation. They are presented more with the provider of the information in mind than its consumer. They are almost always information driven rather than educationally driven in their design, and operate in almost total ignorance of what is known about best practices in the presentation of mathematical data and principles of differential education.[4]

One multigenerational family business had several of its members who were diagnosable with adult attention deficit-hyperactivity disorder. This had significant implications for both how meetings were designed and managed and how materials were presented. Only under the rarest of occasions were spreadsheets used to convey a concept with this family.

Many financial advisors have gotten very creative about how to do this. And there are a variety of tools and techniques that enable advisors to more precisely understand what kind of learners and personalities comprise the system.[5] Some advisory systems, such as the Legacy Wealth Coaching System, urge advisors to use some of these instruments with the broader advisory team as a way to identify the same kinds of data about the advisory team as well. In most cases, however, there is a long way to go toward creating materials that better support the kinds of learning that need to occur.

## Comfort in Talking about Money

On one level, financial advisors are obviously comfortable talking about money with clients. It is exactly what they do day in and out. Well, yes and no. Yes, we are good at talking about alpha and beta investing, tax loss harvesting, Monte Carlo simulations, estate settlement costs, charitable remainder annuity trusts, grantor retained annuity trusts, family limited partnerships, intentionally defective trusts, portfolio construction, asset allocation, income, expenses, universal life policies, long/short investing, capital markets, and the like. The skills listed in Table 8.1 refer to those gaps in our ability to talk about the meaning of money and wealth in the family system. These are the conversations where money loses its abstract and fungible quality and palpably touches participants in the family/advisory system. The ability to discuss highly charged issues, the value of one's own services and the ways conversations should be timed are among key skill areas displayed by the new financial advisor.

## Talking about Charged Money Matters

One family business I worked with had done all the right things. They had attended university-based programs on family businesses, had developed a highly evolved governance system where issues of family ownership and participation could get worked out, and had taken the big step of commissioning an outside board of directors. Moreover, the estate planning was well under way, a family bank was being contemplated to support next-generation entrepreneurship, and the related buy-sell arrangements were in place. Family meetings were sometimes difficult but productive. The family was far from conflict free but had enviable processes in place to manage conflict. The one elephant in the living room did not appear until we began to work on the financial issues in the business. As more information surfaced, it became clear that much of what the family had done did not take into account the fact that the business was not going to be able to fund these grand plans.

Having this conversation with the family was tantamount to having a go-to-treatment conversation with an addict in their deepest state of denial. This meant that the defenses that had built up around this reality were such that the delivery of this message required a carefully choreographed meeting we knew would be extremely painful. But it had to happen and meant at the time that it made no sense to implement some of the financial plans (trusts, insurance policies) we had been contemplating. We were not actually delivering information that was not known to the senior generation. What was happening was that the way in which the senior generation was processing the information (or in a way not processing it) was what we had to pay attention to. We also delivered the message not as unknown data but as data we were processing in different ways and as a different player in the system. On a tactical level, we ourselves had everything to gain by joining in the family's denial. We also had separately built a solution set involving the engagement of a turnaround specialist whom we had begun to source.

Being able to nest bad news in a solution-oriented discourse thus becomes one of those key skill sets that places the advisor truly on the side of the family. In this case, the short-term loss of a tactical sale in the end brought us far closer to the family and positioned us to be the go-to advisor in their system.

## Advisor Compensation and Service Valuation

Once the simple sales of a product no longer becomes your raison d'être opposite your clients, you then traverse into the terrain where one has to talk directly about what other value is being brought in to play for the family. In his training of advisors, Keith Whitaker, of Calibre, acknowledges the difficulty many advisors have in talking about fees. He says that "it is a very emotional issue . . . Most are drawn to the industry to help families [and talking about fees] is something they avoid because it seems to put them in an adversarial position."[6]

This makes complete sense. Advisors are all too human. Even those of us at the Ackerman Institute's Money and Family Life Project[7] had difficulties in our own conversations about the value of what we were doing for the project, what fees we would charge, and what the "house" should have a right to as our sponsor. The art of talking about what a service should cost is primitive and under development in the wealth management industry, with few firms operating outside of the familiar discourse of basis points on assets under management. Some on the advance guard are working more creatively with clients and shifting the conversation more toward a dialogue in which the family participates in helping decide the value of what is being proposed. Rather than supply-side constructs of hourly or per diem compensation, these advisors are altering the conversation around the assignment of value to the outcomes that are being sought. This "value pricing" model is not for the faint of heart. It recalls the "excommunication" of French psychoanalyst Jacques Lacan from the International Psychoanalytic Association for, among other things, telling patients they could pay whatever they wanted for psychoanalysis—as long as they would subject whatever they chose to pay (cash, automobiles, art, vacations) to analysis. This unhooked the value of the process from typical time and money equations and invoked a deeper question of value in the analysand. This made the American psychoanalytic establishment at the time rather nuts, so to speak.

Value pricing does represent one of the most interesting frontiers to explore for the new financial advisor. Imagine the difference in conversations that flow from the different propositions below:

- *Conventional pricing proposition:* "For these planning services, we charge $7,500."
- *Value pricing proposition:* "We will help you organize and plan your family financial affairs, and present you with options designed to optimize your overall family financial functioning—How much might that be worth to you?"

The first conversation anchors the fee to conventional parameters and is perceived as either a good deal or not. The second ups the stakes and invites a more frank exploration of the value of proposed services. It sets a different tone and places responsibility for value creation squarely between client and advisor. The new financial advisor will find him- or herself applying both of these models, depending on the circumstance, but will begin to shift toward value models over time, particularly when the kinds of services that are delivered begin to be experienced as "priceless."

## Sequencing and Pacing Conversations

It is often challenging to know not only how but when to bring up certain topics about money. In general, this can be most easily gauged by running a few "tests" on the topics you are trying to bring up. Some of these might include:

- What in you is determining the urgency level? Is this more about your need or theirs?
- Are there reasons to delay or to accelerate this conversation based on client needs?
- What is the likelihood that this conversation will be fully consumable by the clients?
- What possible fallout can be expected by either delaying or accelerating this conversation?

Once again, we are dealing with capabilities that are more art than science. The best approach to assessing yourself is to look back at critical incidents where you may have mistimed conversations—too early, too late—and ask yourself what the timing drivers were, and whether they were a function of forces you can better understand and manage.

## Family Systems

Simply knowing that whenever you are working with clients they are part of complex systems is a key concept an advisor needs to evolve in his or her own thinking. Greg Rogers, founder of RayLign Advisory, LLC, has developed a matrix that can serve as a reminder of just how complex this system is, in case it is forgotten, which is easy to do when you are caught up in the moment with individual clients. As illustrated in Figure 8.1, it is complicated enough to imagine how embedded a single individual is (looking across the YOU row) in multiple systems. Add generational dimensions to this and you have to potential to be overwhelmed. You

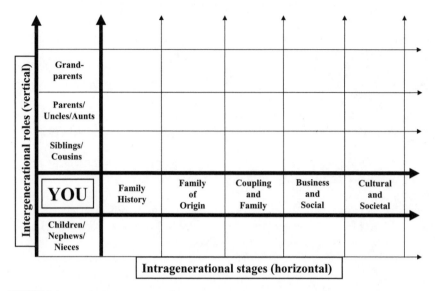

FIGURE 8.1 Family System Complexity

cannot possibly pay attention to all of these variables in your conversations with clients. But you can use grids like this as mnemonic devices in case of need. For our purposes, being able to assess strengths and vulnerabilities in family clients, knowing how to work with subsets of members (a couple, for instance), knowing when to involve others, and the ability to assist in the resolution of conflict all represent an important set of basic skills that can help you differentiate your work with your clients.

## Assessment of Strengths and Vulnerabilities

As in any form of organization, being able to form an assessment of strengths and vulnerabilities of client family systems is key to being able to intervene and embed strategies into these systems that have a chance to be durable. This can be done along a continuum of informal to formal lines, and at this level there is no need to be dogmatic about the means by which you do this as long as it takes into account factors like:

- *History.* Where has this family come from (events, key people, marginalized members, money genogram, etc.)?
- *Structure.* How is the family structured, both informally and formally, as in the case of corporate, philanthropic, partnership, or trust relationships?
- *Governance.* How are decisions made? What checks and balances exist?

- *Individuality.* How well are individual differences tolerated and even encouraged within an overall family identity?
- *Leadership.* What kinds of leadership predominate?
- *Patterns.* What are the relatively predictable ways in which the family responds to challenges? How has it faced challenges and critical incidents?
- *Dynamics.* From the Greek root, *dynamikos,* this term refers quite directly to the "forces" at work in families, whatever they might be.

Rating yourself alone here can be limiting, since it is difficult to know what one doesn't know about how these systems behave and what makes them tick. Going to others to corroborate your self-appraisal is thus very desirable on this variable in particular. Sharing some of your hypotheses and formulations, as well as the data on which they are based, with a peer or supervisor can be extremely instructive.

## Strategic Work with Member Subsets

Because it is extremely rare and not even necessarily desirable to get the whole family across generations in a room together, and because it is even more rare that they would all march into your office and contract with you all at once, working systemically with families is dominated by work with member subsets. Indeed, your work with clients may be dominated by work with an individual for an extended period of time. Assessing yourself along these lines is thus complicated because it really in part involves assessing a mind-set as well as tactics and strategies you deploy using this mind-set. An example of this might involve work that is predominantly with the husband and wife around estate strategies. Many get into trouble here, not just because they neglect to interact with potential beneficiaries as part of their discovery but because they haven't even sorted the dynamic field in which estate planning is taking place through the discourse of the couple in the room. This can involve a failure to sufficiently pick up and explore the roots of ambivalences that emerge in planning conversations.

The plain fact is that you have to get good at imagining, to some extent, the "holography" of the client system as it is manifest in the members proffered up to you for work. What is unique about holograms—and members of client systems—is that each individual image contains the image as a whole. Unlike holograms, where this feature is obvious, individual members often obscure this "whole" that they are a part of, especially in Western cultures pregnant with the ideology of individuality. So, unlike with holograms, I recommend that financial advisors work to see the whole in the individual. Once you are able to do so, then you have to formulate and test perspectives on the whole—how, for instance, you think a particular strategy will be adopted or resisted by members not within your direct reach—and figure out whether direct interactions with other system participants will be needed.

## Determination of Optimal Member Involvement

Clearly related to this is the ability to make judgments about when to involve others. In large measure, what this means for most advisors is that they have evolved a way of working that, when in doubt, begins to shift in favor of including more rather than fewer participants in the work. This does not mean calling a family meeting at the drop of a hat. In many cases, getting permission from your core client to have informational interviews with the kids or grandkids or other advisors in the system is all you need in the early parts of discovery to formulate the nature of involvement that you might want to later orchestrate.

Generally, clients will send you signals about challenges they are having with another participant in their universe. Your job will be to register these signals and determine whether they should be included in the process you have under way and how to choreograph this involvement. This skill involves the ability to do a risk assessment around what it might mean to involve this person in the work. In some cases, your best move may be to involve someone else, such as a family therapist or attorney, to do the work that is needed.

## Conflict Resolution

Assessment of your ability to do conflict resolution in client systems relates in the first instance—as with much in this book—to how *you* handle conflict first, and then extends to how well you help others resolve conflict. Both individuals and systems can generally be assessed according to whether they follow a dominant style out of the following:

- I win/you win.
- We each compromise.
- I win/you lose.
- I lose/you win.
- I lose/you lose.

Generally, it is desirable to start at the top of this list and work your way down toward increasingly less desirable processes. However, some individuals and systems are more locked into one strategy over another, and your ability to influence that may be as important as anything else you do with clients. The fine art of conflict resolution is obviously beyond our treatment here, but this skill should be included among the key skills that you evaluate yourself on. In this area, 360-degree feedback can be particularly helpful.

## Collaboration and Leadership

I can think of fewer constructs as overhyped and underutilized in our industry as collaboration. The ideology of collaboration is compelling enough to make one collude with the tendency to overestimate one's own actual ability to collaborate. I included it here as a way of encouraging new financial advisors to get serious about how truly nested this behavior is in their practices. Collaboration is conflated far too often with the idea of simply making and receiving referrals. Leadership development is not far behind in being one of those constructs that is talked about but underdeveloped in the industry, particularly as it operates at the individual advisor level.

### Alliances with the Family Advisory System

It is fantastical to imagine that you are going to enter a client family without tangling with its advisors. I like to talk about the family advisory system as its own more or less functional or dysfunctional system. Your work with the family is by and large better done with the individual components of that system working in concert than the reverse. In many cases, you will compete directly with at least one extant system participant, even if only in their mind, and that cannot usually be avoided. In more cases, the nature of the competition will be more ephemeral: it won't be so much as, say, one investment manager to another, as it will be a more subtle competition for that position of "most-trusted advisor." You may, for instance, find that as the wealth manager you are strangely tangled in a dance with the chief financial officer in the family business around gaining audience with the patriarch. In other cases, it is an accountant, attorney, or investment advisor who has a palpable stake in what your arrival might mean for their relationship with your client.

The new financial advisor must work in this sublime atmosphere of power and access in order to engage and recruit this system of existing advisors toward ends serving the greater good of the family. The ability to enter the family advisory system effectively and, in some cases, intervene on that system as well as the family system, is far from simple. While the bias of the approach in this book leans toward inclusiveness, a section in the work of Ed and Colette Hoover on *Getting Along in the Family Business* helps unpack the different kinds of collaboration needed in different circumstances, the likelihood of its working, and the pros and cons of each.[8] They chart this along a continuum from simple referral and cross-disciplinary collaboration to multi- and interdisciplinary collaboration, the latter involving a fuller nesting of actual business processes between firms. For assessment purposes, the skill with which you choose and execute the optimal type of collaboration in different circumstances is what is important, not simply a more general assessment of whether you are a good collaborator.

## Wealth Team Leadership

Just as collaboration is fluid and situation dependent, so, too, is the concept of leadership promoted here. I subscribe to a leadership construct in the wealth management environment that draws from Robert Greenleaf, Ken Blanchard, and others that is often referred to as *servant leadership*. So the variables we are looking at are not how controlling, domineering, and unilateral your style is. They are instead related to some of the following:

- Ability to assume the position of stewardship over the resources in his or her purview, not necessarily the position of being their ultimate owner.
- Ability to collaborate.
- Generates trust.
- Is empathic toward others.
- Uses power ethically.
- Creates involvement and esprit de corps.
- Knows when to follow or "get out of the way."

Servant leadership assumes the ability to do these things while keeping an eye on achieving results. This also invokes a notion of leadership that, like being a great coach, has its motivational basis in the desire to help others achieve their best. The great coach is not out on the game field playing ball; he orients all he does toward bringing out excellence in his players. As in any team sport, the trick is in getting greatness through collaboration, not simply through individual stardom.

## Wealth Team Membership

Being a good team member is an important component part, in my view, of being a great leader. In the wealth management theater, this concept ties to the notion that at various times in the life of the family and steps in your strategy, different skills are going to move from background to foreground and vice versa. Whether you are the *de jure* or *de facto* leader of the group, there will be times—in some cases, moment to moment—in which you will need to recede from the limelight in the service of client objectives and team effectiveness. Ideally, you do this in a way that is neither pouty nor belligerent but, in fact, is done with grace and humility.

I know, for example, that bringing someone in to do sophisticated option strategies around a concentrated stock position should not be something I do begrudgingly because I don't have the knowledge or wherewithal to carry this out by myself. In this case, I need to be a confidently silent partner whose job is to make sure this strategy is embedding itself the way it should in the life of the (usually nervous) client. Again, my job is to bring out the best in the team, even if only as a small player in this or that specific process.

## Sourcing and Integration of Expertise

The challenge of this skill set takes the shape of the new problem you are focused on in your business, namely, that of facilitating the overall well-being of the human, intellectual, financial, and social capital of your client systems. This means the horizon of expertise has seriously broadened, and along, in some cases, unfamiliar contours. For example, many advisors may feel that for a wide range of clients they need to somehow have a therapeutic player on the team, but are challenged in several ways to know how to do this. For one thing, how would you know the difference between one family therapist and another? Are the differences between a structural, Bowenian, Milan School, or psychoanalytic therapist clear to you at all? How on earth would you know the difference? How do you really know who is good? And for whom? Assuming you do get into a comfort zone with the provider, how would you ever make a referral? I've spoken to what seem to be legions of financial advisors who are dying to make these kinds of referrals but cannot for the life of them get comfortable with the language of how they would do this without completely spooking, if not insulting, their clients.

Some cases are easier than others. If a family member admits to drug abuse, for instance, the issue is stark and more easily handled on the front end. The implementation end is, of course, easier said than done. Swimming through the sea of providers in the multibillion-dollar drug and alcohol rehabilitation industry remains daunting, even for experts.

More challenging are those border cases where there isn't a palpable pathology screaming for attention. These kinds of instances, about which this entire book is premised, are more subtle zones where psychotherapy is not indicated and where integration with various human capital disciplines becomes a skill set needing to be perfected over time. Many of these disciplines are border players, such as professionals who are, say, wealth psychologists or executive coaches. In many cases, executive coaches are more palatable versions of rebranded psychotherapists drawn to the quadrupling of fees that often attends this rebranding. But branding matters because of, among other things, the loss of the stigma associated with consuming mental health services.

How skilled you are at determining needs and how they will be fulfilled in the complex endeavor that wealth management has become, thus, makes my list of capabilities that new financial advisors should begin assessing in themselves and their firms.

# Integration

Wealth management in the sense we are using it is nothing if not about the integration of many moving disciplinary parts that are not always used to nesting themselves with one another. I break the integration problem down into three basic areas that are in some ways facets of the whole. This includes the ability to analyze human and financial data together, to use this analysis to intervene in the service of family well-being, and to actually use financial strategies as interventions. Because the object of intervention is hybrid capital, that is, the intertwined conglomerate of human, material, and financial capital, the new integration requirements are as challenging as they are palpable.

## Analysis of Human and Financial Data

We spoke earlier of the need for the ability to assess the family system. Here, the challenge is to find ways of more effectively drawing the parallels and intertwined implications for how the wealth system works and is optimized as a complex organism. The medical analogy might further clarify this. Western medicine, like Western financial services, is operating at a crescendo of highly disciplined thinking in its normal functioning. This means that when I go to a physician with an ailment, it had better be quickly identifiable as attached to an organ system or I am in trouble. This means that every effort will be made to determine whether my ailment is a skin problem (go to the dermatologist), a cardiac problem (go to a cardiologist), a skeletal problem (go to an orthopedist), or the like. Heaven help me if my illness crosses organ systems or has psychosomatic analogues. This is the way it is done day to day.

Meanwhile, at the frontier of research and development, the very disciplines of biology, chemistry, and physics are becoming undone at the seams, as in the case where new disciplines like bioinformatics and nanotechnology are beginning to redefine the very way in which, for example, drug delivery systems can work.

The same is true in the advance guard of wealth management, with "postdisciplinary" fields, like behavioral economics, emerging. The challenge in front of most advisors is not unlike that of the physician practicing on the ground. These new rarefied disciplines have yet to work their way through to our day-to-day practices. The integration of financial and human systems data is an emerging skill that needs to make its way out of the universities and into wider use for real advisors and real clients. It will be hard for most of us to mark this skill as "excellent."

## Intervening in the Service of Family Well-Being

Assuming you have done a stand-up job of analyzing and integrating the financial and human systems data, the challenge now becomes how to take this information and reduce it to steps that can be staged in over time and which have a reasonable probability of positively affecting family outcomes. It is one thing to write a stellar, integrated report. It is altogether another thing to convert this to interventions. This becomes the litmus test of our efforts, and as such is distinguished from the ability to simply do the analysis. Knowing what you now know from this integrated analysis, from client system strengths and vulnerabilities and the ways financial flows are affecting family well-being, you now have to make it work in ways that can be measured by variables like client retention. So this measurement dimension is all about your ability to move from discovery through to solution development, implementation, and results management.

## Creative Deployment of Financial Strategies as Interventions

There are many situations in which I have seen therapeutic events orchestrated by nontherapeutic specialists with nontherapeutic strategies. One case I was part of involved a family business with substantial tension emerging around the succession drama that was unfolding in the shadow of a dominant, second-generation leader. What I know about this system is that extreme tension was emerging because there was no apparent way members of the third-generation cousin clan, none of whom were yet successor material for this business, could see how their strengths and desires were fitting with the evolving needs of the business. The concept of procuring a nonfamily, interim CEO was discussed ad nauseam and hands were wrung around how they could possibly generate the incentives necessary both to keep someone who could do the job and reward other nonfamily executives as well. The tension surrounding this did not bring out the best in family members, and they had tried to work through some of the issues with a family therapist. Yet, according to one participant, "in therapy, we were like pilots circling the airport with no hope of landing the plane." The financial planner, circuitously brought in to solve some estate and ownership transition issues, fielded the proposition surrounding the deployment of a "performance unit plan," where one can mimic stock appreciation without driving up business valuations (which pits the owner against the employee for ownership transfer purposes). This plan was funded in large part by a special life insurance arrangement, and had an extraordinary effect on the well-being of the family. They made progress in a short series of meetings that would have been unthinkable using the therapeutic modality alone.

This example demonstrates that any number of what might appear to be "family problems" can sometimes be more profoundly affected by a great financial strategy. Key among them are those that, for example, let the air out of a brewing capital and liquidity tension emerging in families where the dominant asset is an operating business and the shareholders have reached a threshold in either numbers or diversity where their return expectations from the business are in stark conflict. All the family therapy you could buy may never approach the positive effects a new dividend policy, partial public offering, employee stock ownership plan, or private equity infusion might engender in the right circumstances.[9]

This dimension, then, is about the skill with which advisors can more profoundly deploy what they know to solve enormous, seemingly unsolvable problems brought to them by clients.

---

### Tips and Takeaways for the New Financial Advisor

The assessment dimensions listed in Table 8.1 and explicated in the previous pages should be used to generate positive developmental steps that help you better climb into the space where you are able to more effectively enable the achievement of life outcomes in your clients. Together, they represent a tall order, if one believes that they should be scoring an "excellent" in each area. Another way to look at this is to remind yourself that it is okay that you are not perfect in all dimensions. You should set SMART objectives for yourself but also look to your team and partners as supportive players in this newly targeted enterprise. Not only should you not go it alone with respect to your development plan, you should not go it alone with respect to building up your team. Using these dimensions in a 360-like method can start what will be a rewarding and ongoing conversation with your fellow travelers.

# CHAPTER 9

# Ethical Considerations
# for Trusted Advisors

Y ou are going to find yourself staring more, not less, into ethical "gray areas" in doing this work. Period. There are many reasons for this, not the least of which is that you now know that practically everything you do, every bit of advice you deliver, has implications and potential unintended consequences for your clients' lives. This was implicitly true before, but now the gravitas of what you do will resonate even stronger in how you deliver services. And—make no mistake—this is a good thing! Why? Because doing the right thing is both good for the soul and invariably good for business—especially when that business is increasingly based on trust.

In this chapter, I discuss five ethical approaches and the process of making an ethical decision. In doing so, I will discuss how the new financial advisor ought to apply these constructs to their evolving practice. To illustrate these frameworks, I will then provide three case studies. The principals and cases that follow in this chapter will provide guidelines to help you think through scenarios and dilemmas that are increasingly common in the delivery of wealth management services to families.

## Ethical Framework for an Expanded Advisory Frontier

Ethics are not a new area per se for wealth advisors. As members of multiple professional associations, we are obliged to adopt the ethical precepts of those associations. Holding securities licenses, insurance licenses, financial planner designations, and admittances to bar associations each involve acting in ways that, on the surface, are remarkably consistent. The Financial Planning Association could hardly promote an ethics more consistent with the messages in this book when they introduce their code of ethics as follows:

> *From its earliest designs, the Financial Planning Association included a mandate that members will adhere to a code of ethics that reflects their commitment to help clients achieve their life goals.*[1]

This emphasis on the achievement of life goals, and not simply on selling financial products and services in an above-board way, is a theme highly consistent with those in this book.

The focus of this discussion, then, is consistent with the spirit, and usually the letter, of ethical codes that are usually present when one assumes a role in one of the professions underlying the practice of wealth management. The goal here is thus not to repeat the codes but to examine the implications of what is different now that the landscape of your interventions has broadened. We need to ask ourselves if there are new questions we should consider now that we are aware of the larger constituencies we are affecting in our approaches to delivering advice and services.

As in much of ethical thinking and practice, the more difficult issues for us are those that do not lend themselves to crystal-clear resolutions. Under most circumstances, not breaking the law, for example, is de rigueur and ethical codes usually assume a higher standard than just not breaking the law. While brokering subprime mortgages didn't break the law, it could easily place one in problematic ethical terrain. But an estate attorney, for example, even treads in sometimes ambiguous territory when working with a whole family, if only because of the ease with which conflicts of interests and confidentiality breaches can emerge if things don't play out just so. In the estate attorney's judgment, it may make the most ethical sense to involve grantors and beneficiaries in conversations about transfer alternatives, but in some cases they do this under no small peril.

One way to frame our thinking about ethics is to keep our eyes on outcomes that optimize both family and financial decision-making, as is portrayed in Figure 9.1. While optimizing these decisions is far from simple in practice, we should always ask ourselves what is good financially for the family and what is good for the family. Many times, these will not present conflicting scenarios, but estate planners know, for example, that planning that brings the estate tax burden to zero is not always the best solution for the family—the taxes are eliminated but sometimes at the expense of family well-being.

The optimal approach in the ambiguous terrain that lies ahead is probably not to add yet a new ethical code—same as the old code—but instead to raise a set of questions about how the terrain is changing and to generate

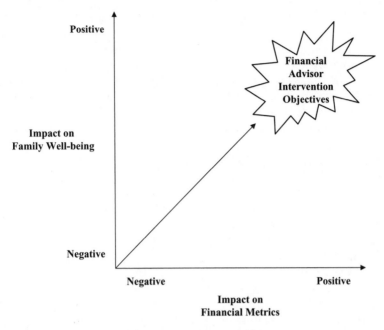

FIGURE 9.1 Optimizing Family Financial Decision Making

an expanding ethical consciousness through dialogue around potentially difficult situations.

## Five Ethical Constructs

With some exceptions, most ethical practice emerges from roughly five lines of thought worth drawing out for our discussions.[2] These include:

- *The utilitarian approach:* This approach seeks, in an imperfect world, to look at the consequences of behavior with respect to the likelihood that more good than harm will be done. Caricatured, this point of view says that if I have a strategy that will harm four out of five people, then it is generally less ethical than one that will harm only one of five people.

    *New financial advisor application*: If an estate transfer strategy hurts only one sibling and his or her lineage, it is better than another strategy that hurts all three children—assuming a common understanding of what "hurt" is.

- *The rights approach.* In this model, action that protects moral or human rights, such as the right to freedom or privacy or not to be injured, is ethical action.

*New financial advisor application:* The question of what age a child has the right to control, know how much is there, or even render a point of view about assets in trust for his or her benefit is far from unusual, including whether such a right can be said to exist at all.

- *The justice approach.* In this approach, the guiding constructs are those of equality and fairness. Where complete equality is not possible, then fairness should at least apply.

  *New financial advisor application:* In passing the shares of the family business to four siblings, the question as to whether shares should be transferred in equal proportions to each child is often weighed against the fairness of such an approach given differing levels of involvement with the business as employees.

- *The common-good approach:* Common-good approaches are those that give rise to rule of law and to the delivery of services, such as fire departments and police forces, which are deemed good because of our basic interconnectedness as members of society.

  *New financial advisor application:* The provision of health insurance for family members or the subsidization of family office services for less financially well-off family members might be instances of this approach in the wealth management space.

- *The virtue approach.* This approach posits ideals of character and action toward which we aspire as ethical beings. These can include courage, compassion, honesty, integrity, and self-restraint.

  *New financial advisor application:* Many families are beginning to ask advisors about how affluence will affect their children's ability to live virtuously in the midst of temptations toward entitlement, toward not working (because they don't have to), and the like. These families are seeking your advice and assistance in the training and propagation of morals and values in their progeny—something well beyond the delivery of financial services.

Integrating components of each of these constructs can provide some guidance to the new financial advisor as we enter the expanded terrain that our new role and value proposition place us. As advisors thinking about client systems rather than simply the individual or couple in front of us, we are challenged to examine the possible consequences of different paths taken on individuals we may never lay eyes on.

## Ethical Decision-Making Process

These five approaches are neither always consistent with one another nor are they applicable in equal amounts in each situation. Since we are also far from perfect ethical actors, what follows is a possible framework where some of the right questions can be asked. We will then examine some paradigmatic cases through the lens of this process. There will be added benefit to using a process like this in a way that is transparent to your clients as well. In most situations, exposing your thought processes to them can act to broaden their own views by surfacing questions they may have not considered. This also has application to the extent that you are also in the business of influencing ethical choices in others, and not simply driving ethical behavior in yourself. This can mean promoting ethical decision making in your clients and also within the institutions in which you work.

Related to this is something you have heard now many times. Namely, do not make decisions having ethical import alone. None of us are smart enough alone to anticipate all the effects of what we set in motion with client systems. Like dropping a pebble in a lake, our interventions ripple out in all directions and beyond our sight lines. Not only are we smarter in teams, it is almost always both better for clients that we process issues this way and better from a risk management perspective.

The following decision process is adapted from the work of the Markkula Center for Applied Ethics at Santa Clara University and spells out several steps integrating the five approaches to ethical decision making:

1. *Recognize the presence of an ethical issue.* Is there something wrong? Is some damage to an individual or group possible? Is the issue beyond institutional rules or legal statutes?
2. *Get the facts.* What are the facts of the case? What facts are missing? How did you come about the facts and verify them? Were sufficient points of view obtained and stakeholders consulted?
3. *Determine the alternatives to be evaluated.* What options are available? Are they sufficiently worked out so they can be evaluated with each other? Is a combination of options possible?
4. *Utilitarian screen.* Which option will produce the most good and do the least harm? (The ethical action produces the greatest balance of benefits over harms.)
5. *Rights screen.* Even if not everyone gets all they want, will everyone's rights and dignity still be respected? (The ethical action is the one that most dutifully respects the rights of all affected.)
6. *Justice screen.* Which option is fair to all stakeholders? (The ethical action is the one that treats people equally or, if not equally, at least fairly.)
7. *Common-good screen.* Which option optimizes the fuller participation in life shared as a family, community and society? (The ethical action contributes most to the achievement of a good, shared quality of life.)

8. *Virtues screen.* Will behaving this way help you become the sort of person you want to be? (The ethical action is one that embodies the highest human values.)
9. *External review.* How will others you respect evaluate the decision you are contemplating?

Generally speaking, working dilemmas through these steps will generate the kind of ethical decision making desired. We can now turn to some case vignettes to try this methodology on.

## Case 1: A Billion to Baby

Chris, the founder of a software company, was being given advice by an estate attorney, as he was approaching the sale of his company for $300 million, to use trusts to shelter sale proceeds in ways that yield substantial tax savings and enable the passage of a huge portion of assets both to his six-month-old son and to his son's children as well. The software entrepreneur was 31 years old and relatively recently married. In spite of making a very handsome income, the couple had remained in the same, modest suburban house and had no plans to move anytime soon. The one splurge he gave in to was to buy a sports car, a purchase over which he seemed more apologetic and shy than proud. As conversations heated up in connection with the coming sale, Chris began to feel a growing sense of unease related to the estate strategy being contemplated. The attorney was pressing hard to get the deal inked so as to capture appreciation potential before the sale. The logic of the transaction seemed impeccable, particularly since Chris had no doubt that he could better put money to use than could the government. It was impossible to argue with the scale of the tax advantages and the economic benefit to his progeny.

However, during one house call by the attorney (house call because a turn of logistical events meant Chris had to stay home with little Kevin, his son), a window into the nature of Chris's unease came as he was holding his son and talking to the attorney. "I realized at that point," recalled Chris, "that I had no concept of what it would mean to make tiny Kevin virtually a billionaire by early adulthood. I had no way to fathom the effects of this on him, his kids, all of us." While holding his young son—whose physical presence drove home the point for Chris and concretized the previously abstract "beneficiary" for the attorney—Chris asked the attorney if he understood why making the irrevocable decisions he was being asked to was giving him pause and keeping him up at night. The effect of seeing the real child put the attorney back on his heels psychologically and his inability to respond meant they had to break off the meeting until the next day.

> *Presence of an ethical issue.* Using the process described above to move through this vignette, we do find that there is an ethical issue emerging between Chris and his attorney. At the heart, Chris is up against a set of irrevocable decisions that will make the young child in his hands colossally wealthy. Although perhaps inarticulate about all his reasons, Chris is resisting the execution of this plan because of thoughts and feelings that are leaving him cold about the deal.
>
> *Get the facts.* Chris and his attorney are probably operating with fewer facts than either of them would like. Some of these are not knowable, such as how little Kevin will react and behave with this wealth when he grows up. We also know that, so far, Chris's wife, Jeanie, may not have weighed in—or may in fact be part of the driver behind Chris's hesitation to move forward. We could also hypothesize that there may be some conflict between the couple about this. For example, Chris could have pushed the attorney unwittingly down the path of this particular strategy simply because he was most used to handling the family's business and financial affairs. The attorney may feel he had drafted a solution that reflected Chris's near phobia of paying taxes only to find his client getting cold feet in the last stretch. The only clear message from Chris might have been to do whatever possible to save taxes. Their design process itself may have unconsciously paid little attention to the human capital effects because the bright light of the money and its ingenious transfer may have blinded both to the other set of questions they might have explored in more depth. The attorney, for example, may have suspected spousal reservations but may not have included her early enough in the process to get a feel for her level of buy-in. Our search for facts here should take us not toward blaming either Chris or the attorney for the predicament, but rather toward looking at the history and circumstances that got them there in the first place and where their might be solutions that take a more encompassing view of the ethical situation.
>
> *What are the alternatives?* In this case, there are likely to be several alternatives with varying timing sensitivities given the oncoming transaction. The clock may run out on some, but the alternatives probably include, at a minimum, doing nothing, taking part of the assets through the strategy, or including additional protective language in the trusts to mitigate certain kinds of fears Chris may have about the effects of this wealth on his children and grandchildren. It can be assumed that there are many possible alternatives that can be advanced, even at this late date.

*Utilitarian screen.* To fully apply this screen, we have to expand the stakeholder universe beyond the immediate attorney, client, and child. The first cycle of this should probably include Jeanie. She is certainly going to have a point of view, and it would be folly to have Chris go further with this by himself. Beyond this, some conversation with parents and any other trusted confidants may provide the attorney with a broadened context in which to view the strategy and make adjustments. At the end of the day, however, the utilitarian screen can only be applied very narrowly because it is only the financial consequence that can be mapped. They would seem to pass this screen well if this is measured by the number of family members who stand to benefit versus those who would be hurt. Whether to broaden the effects of this wealth through philanthropic strategies rather than simply through familial wealth enhancement might be discussed as well: is the greater good being served by passing money only to family members?

*Rights screen.* There do not seem to be any potential rights violations from this strategy. No one seems in danger of harm from this point of view.

*Justice screen.* One approach along these lines may be to clarify whether and to what extent an injustice might be built into the strategy. For example, what will happen if Kevin later has a brother or sister? Will there be inherent inequalities because of an accident of birth order? Similarly, if there are generation-skipping provisions, might the grandchildren end up wealthier than their parents? Is that a dynamic that should be institutionalized? What parenting constructs would Chris and Jeanie need to consider if this were to be the case? There are, then, a set of questions that can help further vet this strategy for its projected fairness to the imaginable parties through time.

*Common-good screen.* We may find in further discovery with the couple that they have latent common-good concerns. There may be nascent but powerful interests in affecting broader than just familial means with this newly found wealth. No doubt the attorney has brought up questions of charity, but they might need to be more deliberately revisited as a possible hidden face of his emerging resistance to the strategy. It is not hard to imagine that the reverse side of Chris's antipathy toward paying taxes is in fact a powerful, if not fully formed, desire to make headway against some social cause or causes and an attendant belief that he could more focus on certain issues than could the government. From the point of view of an ethics discussion, there is enough evidence here to formulate a testable hypothesis about this for the couple.

*Virtues screen.* Interrogating the virtues dimension of this may also generate a more proximal understanding of Chris's and/or Jeanie's resistances to the proposed strategy. It is far from unusual in our culture to imagine a couple like Chris and Jeanie harboring a more or less conscious belief in the fundamental toxicity of inheriting this amount of money. They may feel that this could poison any number of the virtues—hard work, entrepreneurial activity, giving back to society—they want to mature in themselves and cultivate in their children. They may have a palpable fear of entitlement run amok in their kids. The transmission of some core values may feel in jeopardy, even at Kevin's tender age. Values elicitation exercises and financial genograms can tease out the couple's hierarchy of values and point to the origins of any poignant historical drivers of these values, respectively. If the family has never known such vast wealth, they will also be prey to the fabulously ambivalent cultural attitudes toward wealth and overlay these on their own attitudes and values. They may feel, on some level, that no virtues they hold dear will prosper in an environment degraded by extreme wealth.

*External review.* The advising attorney and the couple should consider discussing their situation with trusted outsiders as a way to gain perspective on the decisions they are contemplating. A dialogue with a knowledgeable third party, and/or with other family members or trusted peers, can provide a final screen through which to evaluate such momentous decisions. Sometimes peer resources for families can be found in such organizations as the Family Office Exchange and the Institute for Private Investors. Other organizations, such as Attorneys for Family Held Businesses or the Collaboration for Family Flourishing, can serve as peer resources for advisors around both strategic and ethical consultations. In the end, if Chris, Jeanie, and their advisor feel able to stand up their approach to others whose opinions they respect, they will rest more confidently in their decision.

In this model, the high ground is taken when the family advisory system itself owns the ethical, as well as strategic, dimensions of this kind of decision making. Alternatively, each may attempt to push the other in a suboptimal direction. The attorney may privilege tax savings over the transmission of positive familial values—and may be pushing that way because of partial or false cues from the family signaling that is the way they want to go. The reverse can also be true, where the family is overtly or covertly pushing the advisor to get something done that the advisor's instincts say is wrong-headed from a familial perspective.

## Case 2: The Family Farm

In this case, you are being asked as a financial planner and investment advisor to work with a sibling partnership to develop a strategy around the role of the family farm in their lives and that of their children. Three brothers and a sister, all in their late thirties and early forties, own significant acreage in the area and have a moderately successful farming business. All grew up and worked on the farm, managing different aspects of the business. Their ability to avoid difficulties associated with family farms and consolidations is notable and a source of pride for the family. Further, their well-developed plan enabled the parents, both of whom are deceased, to pass business ownership on with little estate taxation.

The four siblings have lived a good but not lavish lifestyle. They all drive company vehicles and benefit from a good health plan and a growing 401k plan for them and their nonseasonal employees.

One of the brothers has confided in you that there has been an uptick in tension lately, however, because the first set of cousins are approaching college age, and for the first time, there is growing feeling that a cash crunch is on the way. In addition, while most of the cousins have worked on the farm, it is becoming evident that most of them will not do this for a living as adults.

The brother who brought you in has said to you that the question of selling or developing part of the land the family owns has come up because of significant residential real estate development in the area has pushed the value of the land up substantially. This has provoked the most heated discussions he's ever seen among the sibs. One side says, "You cannot destroy Daddy's legacy by selling our land," while the other feels strongly that "there are too many mouths to feed and the business won't support it." This same brother has indicated that his preference is to sell, and he is hopeful you will also be able to design an investment strategy with sale proceeds.

> *Presence of an ethical issue.* To a degree, the preliminary ethical challenges for the advisor are probably configured around whether the advisor can be objective in the delivery of advice and understanding not only who the client is but what stakeholder set is targeted for input and intervention. As in many scenarios having this level of complexity, the problem is often right against right rather than where there is a clear set of good guys and bad guys. So while there may not be any stark ethical issues out of the ordinary, the set of ethical questions that can be raised may indeed support a more thorough discovery process. This in turn will heighten the probability that what you recommend will actually be adopted by the family.

*Get the facts.* The facts of the case are likely to point to land valuations that well outstrip the value of the farming business. In assessment of preferences and values, the reported differences between the two factions will probably be borne out, with greater detail on how strongly certain members feel about their positions. The sale of land will bring in a substantial amount of liquidity, but the way of life and career aspirations of some would be blown to the wind by a sale.

*What are the alternatives?* The alternatives probably run a range, from outright or partial sales to outside parties, to some form of internal branch buyout, to some other form of loan or recapitalization program that would free up some amount of liquidity to those who need it. That is, there may be alternatives that stand between all-or-nothing sales proposals, but these may still leave ill feelings because they won't perfectly sync with stakeholder needs. Developing financial strategies that support the evolution and diversification of shareholder needs will play a crucial role in this case. It will not likely be enough to imagine that if there were just better communication or more goodwill spread around that the ethical alternatives can be developed. Sending the family to a family therapist, for example, to get along better will probably not be on the list of alternatives, at least by itself.

*Utilitarian screen.* This screen will again expand the stakeholder universe beyond the brother who has made contact and who has a strong likelihood of using the investment management services of the financial advisor. It is clear that the effects of virtually any financial transaction will affect two generations of siblings and cousins. The utilitarian screen by itself poses both a numbers game—how can the most stakeholders benefit from advisory actions—and a question about the nature of the benefits sought. That is, maximizing the financial benefits to as many as possible may still leave open the question of maximizing the psychological benefits to the greatest number. Many times, these two track nicely. The utilitarian screen can provide a gap analysis between these two types of benefits and might best be executed via some kind of formal or informal survey methodology.

*Rights screen.* As usual, the rights screen begs the question concerning what rights should exists in the family above legal rights of joint ownership. In some cases, this could be a context for developing a "family constitution" that spells out these rights for family members. Are there, for example, rights to vote on possible transaction scenarios and at what age do these rights vest? The advisor may have time to build this project out with the family given that the needs being expressed are not pressing. For example, the right to the "pursuit of happiness" is a familiar right that, as in the U.S. Constitution, is granted but not funded. Expanding this construct out with the family might involve the determination of under what circumstances family members have rights to educational funding and other comparable rights. Thus, an argument can be made out of the rights framework that the rights and responsibilities of being a part of this family should be articulated in advance of, or at least alongside, any financial strategy that is worked out.

*Justice screen.* The advisor is hardly obliged by his or her ethical codes to do anything other than advocate for the fairness of the solution for his initial client. This may evolve to as simple a solution that a sale is made and the proceeds are divided equally. To the extent that there was uneven participation, they might even decide that a more fair allocation can be derived. As the stakeholder set enlarges to even potentially include the cousins, however, questions of fairness could take the form of "to each according to their need," though the psychological calculus for this could be complex and require sustained facilitation by the advisor.

*Common-good screen.* There may be other factors, such as the family's interest in a certain kind of cohesion, that might appear on this screen. The family has a history of working together and making decisions around the farm. Their ability to imagine a future where joint ties and decision making will take place along the same lines as before will be challenged. The common-good question might take the form of whether there are in fact any reasons the families should maintain similar ties in the absence of holding and working joint assets. There may be postsale opportunities for family buying power to be consolidated, say, in the form of an investment partnership. But does this or some other practice answer the common-good questions? Other types of common-good questions might be raised to the extent that a different allocation of proceeds might be made on the basis of a cousin's having a pervasive developmental disorder or disability. The question could be asked about whether, for example, a special-needs trust should be collectively funded in order to support the communal feelings associated with how they take care of each other as an allied community. Whether the family actually retains common-good sentiments or wants to scatter to the wind, the advisor does the ethical thing by at least asking the questions required to tease this out.

*Virtues screen.* In this case, it may well be that the collision between those who want to sell and those who view even the idea as a desecration of their father's will represents the collision between

utilitarian and virtues-oriented values and ethics. The virtue of honoring one's elders may be the tip of the iceberg when it comes to
the ethical values that permeate a multigenerational farming enterprise. These might include hard work, community service, frugality,
and honesty. If the projected transition has no answer to this dimension of values, the wheels may come off the transaction itself. The
advisor should be alert that in a family business with this longevity,
these virtues are more lived and practiced than articulated. They
have been embedded in everyday life by the nature of the family
enterprise. When the mechanism that has tied these practices together is in danger of passing from the family, the advisor should
not assume that the family will know how to articulate its values in
its absence. Consciously or not, the family will also feel the coming
threat to these values as the transition from enterprise family to rich
family looms large in all its connotations. The advisor's job here is
to help surface the family's values scheme as a way of helping them
initiate a transition without loss of the moral and values compass
that has guided them thus far.

*External review.* The more obvious reason for an external review is
to validate the advisor's suitability for working this job given that
he or she may have a financial stake in certain kinds of resolutions over others. But the more interesting backdrop for getting
peer review and/or additional help on the case is the complexity of
the issues embedded in this client system. The many moving parts
representing the human and financial dimensions—and the potential skill sets needed to even do effective discovery and solution
development—make it practically unethical to try to go this alone.
The stakes are too high, as measured by the lives affected. Moreover, arriving on the scene with only a financial perspective will
limit not only the ethical vision needed but may bog down decision
making because of the permeation of the projected transition with
significant human-side considerations.

Using the ethical screens here can bolster effectiveness and add insurance that the solution developed is one with substantial buy-in.

## Case 3: The Financial Outing of Jerry

You are an investment professional, and one of your current clients, Camille,
is quite satisfied with her $1.5 million in investments with you, particularly
since her portfolio has held steady even through recent volatility. She has
made an appointment with you and over the phone indicated that she was

changing her estate planning, and would like to bring over more assets for you to manage inside a charitable remainder trust (CRT). She indicates to you that these other assets, currently managed by one of your competitors, are in the $2 million range.

When she arrives at her appointment, she tells you the following:

- She has recently been devastated to find that 17-year-old Jerry, her only child, is gay and she intends to cut him out of her estate.
- Her husband does not know she is going to give her money to charity, but it is hers to give.
- The charitable trust has already been drafted and she will be bringing copies and other documentation so that you can immediately open the account and fund the new charitable strategy.

*Presence of an ethical issue.* Tradition might suggest, with some credibility, that the advisor really has no special ethical conundrum here. Arguably, there is reason to assume that a client has made an adult decision and that it would hardly be the place of the advisor to do anything other than take the order—and a handsome one at that. Recall, too, Jay Hughes's description of the *personne d'affaires* as someone who does just that: acts as a purveyor of financial goods and services. Recall as well his notion of the *personne de confiance,* who is not simply one in the business of order taking, but rather of assisting clients in their broader journey of wealth as we have defined it. In this latter framework, we can imagine that there is the potential for ethical concerns that lurk beneath the simple requested transaction and that the advisor might make fruitful use of the ethical decision-making process to clear any potential problems.

*Get the facts.* In your interview, you may augment any typical questions you might ask with some of the following to gain greater clarity about what you are being asked to participate in:
  - Is Camille acting within her own ethical framework, or is she being pulled from it by her grief? For example, does she normally abide by the principle of unilateral action without her husband's awareness?
  - What made her fire the other investment advisor? Is it simply performance or service related, or is it tied to this precipitous event?
  - Is there a potential step you may be asked to take that would violate your own ethical codes or values?
  - Will a greater harm to the client system occur if you simply take the order?

- What concerns, if any, came up from the attorney drafting the trust? What made the CRT the vehicle of choice? How did the previous estate plan work? Are there other trusts with other purposes?
- How close have mother and son actually been? Would he have had any expectation of an inheritance anyway, and would he have even wanted it? What does she believe his frame of mind is now?
- Where is Dad in all this? How much does he know about the son? What will his reaction be upon finding out that such a transaction has occurred?

In this case, getting the facts is more than a trivial exercise and may also test the relationship. Indeed, what relationship framework has already been established between you and Camille, not to mention between you and her husband and Jerry? From a cinematic perspective, she's let you view the trailer, but is she asking you to be part of the full motion picture? What role has she in mind for you? Butler or concierge? Or the one who's going to call her to task and insist that she bring hesitation and review to the irrevocable decision she is contemplating?

*What are the alternatives?* Without fuller answers to these questions, you will be hard pressed to find alternatives that might even allow for less "irrevocability" in what she is about to do. One rarely makes a great decision when angry or hurt at the apparent level exhibited by Camille. But she did arrive at the use of a CRT over other options her attorney surely presented her, and there must be a logic to it, however based in high-test feelings. Certainly, doing nothing is an option worth suggesting while the air is let out of the emotional balloon that appears to be driving the transaction.

*Utilitarian screen.* On the face of it, it is hard to determine the extent to which the greatest good for the greatest number is being done here. Perhaps Camille is doing just that by diverting assets away from her son and making them go to work through charitable projects. In this case, the balance shifts from a utilitarian perspective in favor of the reach that may be obtained through charitable giving. Inside the family itself, it is far from clear that the greater number of the three members will benefit from this transaction, and, from a family dynamics perspective, the negative blowback potential of such a decision could be divisive and lasting.

*Rights screen.* Few would argue that children have anything like inalienable rights to inheritances. More might argue that the right of a

husband to know about a decision of this magnitude is common-
place. But we don't as yet know the relationships between the parties or whether, for example, Camille is estranged from her husband.
The question to her about whether she thinks others should have
any rights concerning the transaction she's contemplating might
prove productive along these lines, but the likelihood in this state
that she believes anyone else has any rights over this money is slim
to none.

*Justice screen.* The concern for equality or fairness on Camille's part
seems limited from the point of view of the fact pattern above. But
an interesting act of punishment does seem under way in Camille's
proposed actions. This may mean that some other unfairness is
being answered. Is it unfair that she ended up with a gay son in
her framework? What familial contract was violated? Was a reli-
gious exigency transgressed? Is the remainderman charity antigay
and therefore part of the criminal rectification? Whatever it was,
does the punishment fit the crime? Though strange on the surface,
these "judicial" questions might actually enable a more thoughtful
conversation about the significance of what is being contemplated.
Sometimes it is in precisely the symbolism of justice that deeper
motives are nested. Dynamically, there is also a strong chance that
Camille is either developing or in full sway of a transference to the
advisor that will put you in the role of judge. If this is true, her
approach to you will be marked by her questioning and testing
you as to whether you are on her side or not. You may develop
a feeling that she is presenting to you as if in the midst of oral
arguments in court. We have enough suspicion that some form of
justice is being meted out, even though it may not at all place us in
an ethical conundrum as advisors per se.

*Common-good screen.* It is hard to imagine that the common good of
the family is being addressed by these actions if they are taken as
indicated and without further information about what is really going
on. By wresting away her son's inheritance, Camille may feel this
is doing more good for the real or imagined community she is a
part of. This is worth exploring, as would be the real effectiveness
this gesture is likely to have in accomplishing this objective. As
an advisor, you may also feel the same way. She may, indeed,
have sought you out as someone she could expect to support this
construct. In this view, the community is better off if Camille diverts
funds to, say, the Boy Scouts, than into the hands of her sinful son.
Either way, the common familial good may suffer more from the
way this gesture is being made (unilateral and with no transparency

to the husband) than in the decision itself. This will be among the issues you can raise along the way.

*Virtues screen.* This case, as others we have looked at, may well have its trickiest flashpoints at the intersection of values differences among all the parties in the family advisory system. Clashing ideas as to what counts as virtuous action can threaten this family's integrity and the tie between the advisor and the family. As an advisor, you are going to be put in a situation in which your loyalty to Camille is going to be tested against other values you hold. You may have little sympathy to what Camille is about to do to her son. Or you may feel even stronger about it—so much so that you feel her reasoning violates an internal code you have about the fair treatment of anyone, regardless of their sexual orientation. Equally, your hot button might be Camille's failure to tell her husband. You may have worked with them as a couple, which would place you in a highly problematic relationship with Camille's husband were you to simply go along with this. Honesty and transparency may be virtues you hold too dear to surrender. Similarly, you may hold that the virtuous actor does not collude with a client who may be putting her family relationships on the rocks with a gesture made in anger. As alluded to earlier, you may feel that it is also inconsistent with virtuous action to collude with your client, acting in a way that you know is outside their own value system. Camille may in every respect be a "different person" under the stress and symbolism of her son's revelation. If this is true, presenting feedback to that effect can give you a window into how she is really processing this experience and how it can be further explored.

*External review.* The most important reason to review this kind of case with an outsider is not only for technical or tactical insight. Rather, the most important reason to review this case is under the circumstance that it calls out a lot of feeling on your part as the advisor. Being placed in the positions you have been opposite each family member can be tricky at best and potentially disastrous. You may have very strong reactions to what you're being asked to do, including the crossing of lines you may have never been asked to cross before. Given the volatility of this situation, it is not only prudent to get a quick consult before Camille shows up but also to build in the possibility of taking a "time-out" when she is there and once you have gathered more data. I have often told clients I need a time-out to review and think about what I want to do, and when I do this unapologetically, I usually find that clients appreciate that I am that thoughtful around their concerns to do so.

## Tips and Takeaways for the New Financial Advisor

If there is a major takeaway from this ethics discussion, it should be this: not only is making ethics a day-to-day part of how you work the right thing to do, it can also make you more effective. The questions ethicists raise for us can help us think more deeply and broadly about our actions and what we are preventing or supporting in our client systems. They teach us prudence about looking at the ripple effects through larger stakeholder sets, and this makes us better at thinking systemically about our clients. They invite us to think past the present tense and toward potential unintended consequences of actions we support. Our knowledge that we are affecting the lives of more than the one or two people currently sitting in our office requires of us a greater responsibility opposite the larger *system* we are affecting.

There is thus no downside in my view to evolving the ethical constructs we use as our role gains in importance in our clients' lives. There are fewer extra efforts I can think of that can pay the kinds of dividends that this kind of thinking and acting pays. This is for our clients and ourselves.

This thinking is a work in progress. Far from having a final word on the topic, this chapter is meant to stretch you beyond the basic codes of the professions in which you serve. It is meant to supplement and foster the discussion of what now is needed in the new role you are assuming for your clients. It is meant to enhance your skill set and understanding of what it means to be a new financial advisor.

# Tools for Engaging and Changing Families

This appendix lists various instruments and tools that financial advisors use to engage families around issues that may affect financial and family well-being. The scope of listed items excludes highly technical instruments used with individuals and families, such as those designed to assess serious pathology. It also excludes, for the most part, equally technical financial devices, such as tools for running complex financial simulations. In general, the tools listed below are accessible on the open market or through some qualification or certification method where a modest amount of training is required.

TABLE A.1  Instruments and Tools for Working with Families

| Item | Purpose | Publisher | Observations |
|------|---------|-----------|--------------|
| Values card sorts | Assistance in generating conversations with families around difficult financial topics. | C/O Judith Stern Peck Ackerman Institute for the Family 149 East 78th Street New York, NY 10075 Telephone: 212-879-4900 ackerman@ackerman. org | Two card sorts: one for content values, one for process values. Content values include, for example, financial independence and self-improvement; process values include, for example, inclusiveness and transparency. Useful with individual families and workshop settings for families and advisors. |
| Family Business Inventory assessment tools (family business and family wealth versions) | Each inventory is a 100-short-answer question tool that gathers information about different perceptions of family members concerning the family, its business, and the management of its assets and wealth. Each one has 5 scales with 10 questions in each scale. | Aspen Family Business Group 5608 Malvey Avenue Suite 204 Fort Worth, Texas 76107 Telephone: 866-442-7736; or contact Joe Paul at either 503-297-0750 or at familyfirm@aol.com; http://www.aspen familybusiness.com/inventory. htm. | Advisors administer this tool to the whole family and are able to identify in a nonthreatening way areas of agreement and disagreement among family members, whether the underlying wealth is an operating business or financial assets. |

| Tool | Description | Contact | Notes |
|---|---|---|---|
| Family Enterprise Leadership System (FELS) | FELS provides an objective, confidential and comprehensive method to cultivate the leadership abilities and potential of key participants in family enterprises. | Relative Solutions, LLC<br>Contact: Fran Lotery, Ph.D.<br>13650 Marina Pointe Drive<br>Marina Del Rey, CA 90202<br>Telephone: 310-822-8401<br>flotery@relative-solutions.com;<br>http://www.felsystem.com/. | Leading instrument using 360-degree methods to help families assess and develop leaders in alignment with organizational needs. |
| Family Business Survey | Identifies areas of perceived differences among members of business-owning families. | Contact: Drew Mendoza,<br>mendoza@efamilybusiness.com<br>Telephone: 770-421-0110<br>http://efamilybusiness.com/fep-tools.survey.php | This tool has been in use since 2000 and is Web based. |
| Legacy Wealth Optimization System and Discovery software | Comprehensive values-based tools, methods and supporting software focused on helping couples and families develop vision, goals and mission in a way that in turn drives the development of financial blueprints in the context of complexity and risk tolerances; also helps with project and wealth team management. | The Legacy Companies, LLC<br>99 Derby Street Suite 203<br>Hingham, MA 02043<br>Telephone: 781-740-0033<br>info@legacyboston.com<br>Fax: 781-740-0553;<br>This e-mail address is being protected from spam bots; you need JavaScript enabled to view it. www.legacyboston.com/index.php?option=com-frontpage&Itemid=1 | Very useful toolset for assisting in Discovery, especially with couples who may not yet be completely on the same page with respect to allocations between financial independence, family inheritance, and social capital. |

*(Continued)*

**TABLE A.1 Instruments and Tools for Working with Families (*Continued*)**

| Item | Purpose | Publisher | Observations |
|---|---|---|---|
| Structure of Intellect (SOI) | SOI is designed to assist in the assessment of learning styles, something that is often highly variable across family members | Contact Valerie Maxwell, PhD, 2007 Cedar Ave. Manhattan Beach, CA 90266 Telephone: 310-546-6500 #1 Fax: 310-546-9068 ADDSOI.com LearningGymUSA.com | Dr. Maxwell has used SOI and other devices in wealth management as well as clinical spaces and can provide developmental services for both children and adults. |
| 4MAT | Another learning style system, 4MAT can help the advisor develop learning approaches that are more sensitive to issues such as hemisphere dominance in family members. | Bernice McCarthy About Learning 4MAT SYSTEM 441 West Bonner Road Wauconda, IL 60084 Toll free: 800-822-4628 www.aboutlearning.com | Four types of learners are characterized as being predominantly interested in Why, What, How, and If questions. The simplicity of the system is a strength. |
| Enneagrams | The enneagram is a set of personality instruments that help an individual, team or family describe their personalities in one of nine types. | The Enneagram Institute World Headquarters 3355 Main St., Route 209 Stone Ridge, NY 12484 Telephone: 845-687-9878 Toll free in the United States: 888-Enneagram or 888-366-3247 Fax: 845-687-7486 www.enneagraminstitute.com | The core instrument is the Riso-Hudson Enneagram Type Indicator, though there are scaled-back versions and card sorts. |

| UIF Discovery™ | UIF Discovery™ helps individuals navigate professional direction and facilitate personal change through a dynamic process of self-discovery and insight. | The Uncommon Individual Foundation<br>919 Conestoga Road<br>Building Two, Suite 207<br>Rosemont, PA 19010<br>Telephone: 610-520-0180<br>Fax: 610-520-0188<br>www.uncommonindividual foundation.org | A number of advisors have found this to be an adjunctive process useful for synchronizing an individual's needs and motivations with career and vocational choices. |
| Herrmann Brain Dominance Instrument (HBDI) | Published by Herrmann International, the HBDI is a 120-question assessment that identifies your preferred approach to thinking along the lines of whether an individual is more emotional, analytical, structural, or strategic in how they work. | Herrmann International<br>794 Buffalo Creek Road<br>Lake Lure, NC 28746<br>Telephone: 828-625-9153<br>Toll free: 800-432-HBDI [4234]<br>Fax: 828-625-1402<br>info@hbdi.com;<br>www.hbdi.com/home/index.cfm | This instrument is not only useful for individuals but also works well with families, teams and organizations. Certification is required. |
| DISC® Profiling | The DISC Personal Profile System is personality behavioral testing profiling using a four-dimensional model of normal behavior in an assessment inventory, and survey format in both self-scored paper or online versions. | Inscape Publishing<br>c/o Mills & Associates, LLC<br>Dr Jennie Mills, PhD<br>P.O. Box 11238<br>Arrowhead Station<br>AZ 85318-1238<br>www.DiscProfile.com and<br>www.DiscProfiles.com | DISC has been around for several decades and provides behaviorally based assessments of Dominance, Inducement (Influence), Steadiness (Submission), and Conscientiousness (Compliance). This tool can be used with individuals and families as a whole. |

*(Continued)*

**TABLE A.1  Instruments and Tools for Working with Families** (*Continued*)

| Item | Purpose | Publisher | Observations |
|---|---|---|---|
| Intergenerational Questionnaire: Creating Pathways | The Intergenerational Questionnaire is a tool for personal reflection and for use in facilitating family discussions about themselves and wealth. | Thayer Willis MA, LCSW<br>Thayer Willis, LLC<br>340 Oswego Pointe Drive, Suite 205<br>Lake Oswego, Oregon 97034<br>Telephone: 503-636-1179<br>Fax: 503-244-9410<br>tw@thayerwillis.com<br>www.thayerwillis.com | This tool was written from from both the author's clinical experience and experience growing up in a wealthy family. |
| Values 360 | This tool can help individuals identify five core values in a free, online assessment process that can then be given to others in the family to gather data on consistency between how the individual is viewed by himself versus others. | Lennick Aberman Group<br>Rick Aberman, PhD<br>Telephone: 952-595-4497<br>aberm001@umn.edu or<br>www.lennickaberman.com | Helps assess discrepancies between ideal or espoused values and how they are really implemented. |
| Family Development Matrix | The Family Development Matrix is a tool designed to help family support caseworkers measure the progress of the families they serve. | Jerry Endres California State University<br>Monterey Bay Institute for Community Collaborative Studies<br>100 Campus Center, Building 86 D<br>Seaside, CA 93955<br>Telephone: 831-582-3624<br>jerry.endres@csumb.edu | Though designed for use in a very different context, this device can help wealth managers assess and characterize progress along varying dimensions of family life and can be customized for use in specific circumstances. |

| *Family Assessment: Tools for Understanding and Intervention* (book) | Though it has a mental health focus, this book provides a practical, easy-to-use guide for pinpointing the strengths and limitations families have for dealing with a range of issues. | The author is Adele M. Holman, and her books are available from all major booksellers. | Holman discusses elements crucial to understanding a family—the family as a system, the family and its environment, and the family life cycle. She explains such tested methods for assessing family problems as ecomaps, genograms, family sculpture, the use of observation and checklists, and shows how family assessment lays the groundwork for effective intervention planning. Helpful features include case studies, exercises, charts, and sample forms. |

# Training and Resources
# for Advisors

This appendix lists a number of training programs and other resources that can be helpful to advisors in their efforts to become more sophisticated practitioners with families. These programs and resources aren't always focused on families per se but train on some of the components that can enhance this work and your ability to have stronger, deeper relationships with clients.

**TABLE B.1** Training Programs and Resources for Advisors

| Program | Description | Contact |
|---|---|---|
| The Discovery Institute, The Legacy Wealth Coach Program and The Legacy Wealth Coach Network | These tiered programs concentrate on helping advisors operate as the "most trusted advisor" to their clients. They concentrate on tools, techniques, and business model components that support this kind of practice. | The Legacy Companies, LLC 99 Derby Street, Suite 203 Hingham, MA 02043 Telephone: 781-740-0033 Fax: 781-740-0553 info@legacyboston.com This e-mail address is being protected from spam bots; you need JavaScript enabled to view it www.legacyboston.com/index.php?option= com.frontpage&Itemid=1 |
| Certified Wealth Mentor Program | This program is designed to help advisors incorporate coaching, education, and leadership skills into their advisory practice. The program uses the firm's Financial DNA® profiles, facilitation tools, mentoring and education in support of these objectives. | FinancialDNA® 3340 Peachtree Road NE, Suite 1800 Atlanta, GA 30326 Telephone: 404-812-5318 Fax: 404-812-5374 qualitylife@financialdna.com www.financialdna.com/advisor/Default.aspx? PageID=5&ParentID=5&Level=1 |
| Money, Meaning and Choices Institute (MMCI) | MMCI has training and licensing programs for financial advisors that focus on creating "a better understanding of the interface between psychological and financial issues." | Money, Meaning and Choices Institute P.O. Box 803 Kentfield, California 94914 Telephone: 415-267-6107 mmcinstitute@mindspring.com; www.mmcinstitute.com/index.html |

| Registered Life Planner® | This curriculum augments advisor training in connection with the Life Planning movement. Based on George Kinder's books, *The Seven Stages of Money Maturity* and *Lighting the Torch: The Kinder Method of Life Planning*, training for Registered Life Planner® is implemented over a five-day period that emphasizes that you have to have used the method on yourself before you can fully do this kind of life financial planning with others. | Kinder Institute of Life Planning<br>P.O. Box 1350<br>Littleton, MA 01460<br>Telephone: 978-486-8053<br>Fax: 978-486-8750<br>Eva Brodzik, Director of Business Development<br>Office: 913-232-7506<br>Mobile: 913-709-7689<br>eva.brodzik@kinderinstitute.com<br>www.kinderinstitute.com |
| Advisor Fire Drills | Custom training modules that help advisors anticipate certain kinds of transitions are available around the following themes: sudden death, aging families, health care, and unexpected wealth. These are based on books on the same themes from the consultants at Transition Dynamics, Inc. | Bonnie Brown Hartley<br>Transition Dynamics, Inc.<br>101 West Venice Avenue, Suite 10<br>Venice, FL 34285<br>Telephone: 941-480-1119<br>Fax: 941-484-5702<br>bbh@transdyninc.com |
| Values-Based Financial Professional™ | Bachrach & Associates, Inc. provides a number of tactical and ongoing training and coaching services centered around their core values–based approach to the advisory business. This approach is also articulated in several books by Bill Bachrach, including *High Trust Leadership, It's All About Them*, and *Values-Based Financial Planning*. | Bachrach & Associates, Inc.<br>8380 Miramar Mall, Suite 200<br>San Diego, California 92121<br>Telephone: 858-558-3200<br>Toll free: 800347-3707<br>Fax: (858) 558-0748<br>www.bachrachvbs.com/index.html |

*(Continued)*

**TABLE B.1  Training Programs and Resources for Advisors (*Continued*)**

| Program | Description | Contact |
|---|---|---|
| Ackerman Institute for the Family | Ackerman provides facilitation training in one-day workshop formats, including Facilitating Conversations, Facilitating Family Meetings, and Working with Family Businesses. | Judith Stern Peck Ackerman Institute for the Family 149 East 78th Street New York, NY 10075 Telephone: 212-879-4900 ackerman@ackerman.org |
| Financial Life Planning | Mitch Anthony has several training offerings and tools geared toward helping advisors ask better questions of their clients in order to find out what their deeper desires and needs are from life. Some of these concentrate primarily on selling, but others are focused on use of tools and development of practice capabilities as well. | www.Mitchanthony.com |
| 360 Practices | Workshops offered by 360 Practices concentrate on family and owner-managed businesses but educate about a number of highly relevant issues related to the "human capital" side of wealth. | David Cohn Telephone: 303-771-9929 david@davidcohn.net www.360practices.com/index.php |
| Working with Families of Wealth | This is a workshop for advisors that focuses on family dynamics, family systems, and money issues over the course of four days. | Charles Collier, Harvard University 124 Mount Auburn Street Cambridge, MA 02138 Telephone: 617-495-5218 ccollier@harvard.edu |

| Certificate in Family Wealth Advising | Goals for this certificate are stated as follows:<br>• To educate applicants on the complexity of enterprising families.<br>• To provide applicants with resources to use with families going through the transition from an operating business to a wealth-generating enterprise.<br>• To educate applicants on the family decision process.<br>• To assist applicants in developing advisor collaboration.<br><br>This certificate requires as a prerequisite (or sometimes as a corequisite) completion of the Certificate in Family Business Advising. | The Family Firm Institute, Inc.<br>200 Lincoln Street, #201<br>Boston, MA 02111<br>Telephone: 617-482-3045<br>Fax: 617-482-3049<br>ffi@ffi.org www.ffi.org |
| Institute for Private Investors (IPI) | Though primarily focused on the owners of financial assets, IPI conducts advisor roundtables and provides access to member research on its family members. Occasionally, the focus extends to family dynamics and related issues. | Institute for Private Investors<br>17 State Street<br>New York, NY 10004<br>Telephone: 212-693-1300<br>Fax: 212-693-2797<br>www.memberlink.net |

(Continued)

**TABLE B.1** Training Programs and Resources for Advisors (*Continued*)

| Program | Description | Contact |
|---------|-------------|---------|
| Investor Education Collaborative, IEC | Founded in 2004, the Investor Education Collaborative, IEC, is an affiliated company with IPI. IEC was inspired by 17 years' experience in providing neutral investor education—both at hundreds of IPI events since 1992 and during the past nine years of the Private Wealth Management program at Wharton. IEC uses a case study library, case formats, and learning objectives for programs that are all tested with investors. Each case runs for 90 minutes and is designed for groups of as few as 4 or as many as 12 participants. More than 12 can participate at one time if separate teams are set up. This engaging and highly interactive format offers a chance for the participants to deepen their understanding of one another and themselves. When done within an advisor or money manager's client meetings, it is particularly powerful because the advisors and investors learn together. | Investor Education Collaborative 17 State Street New York, NY 10004 Telephone: 212-693-1300 Fax: 212-693-2797 www.investoreducationcollaborative.com |
| Family Office Exchange (FOX) | As with IPI, FOX offers some educational support to advisors through roundtable and seminar events. Also available is a comprehensive reading list with summaries that covers several areas related to family governance, family business, and broader family issues, as well as more traditional topics. | Family Office Exchange 100 S. Wacker Drive, Suite 900 Chicago, IL 60606 Telephone: 312-327-1200 Fax: 312-327-1212 www.foxexchange.com/public/fox/welcome/ |
| Loedstar | Loedstar provides seminars to advisors on working with family enterprises that touch on a number of themes we've discussed. | Loedstar S.A. 72 boulevard de Saint-Georges, 1205 Geneva, Switzerland Enquiries: +41 22 328 4610 Fax: +41 22 328 4611 www.loedstar.com/ |

# Notes

## Introduction: Where We Are and How It Got That Way

1. This has been stressed most recently in the prestigious CapGemini/ Merrill Lynch World Wealth Report, 2007, where one of its three major sections is entirely devoted to "Adopting a New Service Model for HNW Clients."
2. See a description of Calibre's family dynamics practice at http:// calibre.com/pages/0,,3063_11098,00.html.

## Chapter 1: Accepting the Challenge

1. G. S. Budge, "Continuing Challenges to Delivering Integrated Wealth Management Services to Business Owners." *Journal of Wealth Management* 10 (2007): 51–62.
2. K. Kaye, "When the Family Business Is a Sickness." *Family Business Review* 9 1996, 347–368.
3. Budge, "Continuing Challenges to Delivering Integrated Wealth Management Services to Business Owners," 51.
4. Interview with Keith Whitaker, PhD, of Wachovia's Calibre unit, September 7, 2007.

## Chapter 2: The Psychology of Money and Wealth

1. D. Kahneman, "Maps of Bounded Rationality: Psychology for Behavioral Economics." *American Economic Review* 93 (2003): 1449–1475.
2. G. Belsky and T. Gilovich, *Why Smart People Make Big Money Mistakes—and How to Correct Them: Lessons from the New Science of Behavioral Economics* (New York: Simon & Schuster, 1999).
3. www.lsvasset.com/jsps/about/investphilo.jsp.
4. R. A. Prince and K. M. File, Cultivating the Affluent: How to Segment and Service the High-Net-Worth Market (New York: Institutional Investor, 1995).

5. J. S. Peck, *Money and Meaning* (Hoboken, NJ: John Wiley & Sons, 2007).

6. J. W. Schott, *Mind Over Money: Matching Your Personality to a Winning Financial Strategy* (Boston: Little Brown, 1998).

7. Interview with Keith Whitaker of Wachovia's Calibre unit, September 7, 2007.

8. R. H. Thaler, "Towards a Positive Theory of Consumer Choice. *Journal of Economic Behavior and Organization* 1 (1980): 39–60.

9. Cf. Richard H. Thayler, *The Winner's Curse: Paradoxes and Anomalies of Economic Life* (Princeton, NJ: Princeton University Press, 1992).

10. Belsky & Gillovich, *Why Smart People Make Big Money Mistakes—and How to Correct Them*, 37.

11. Cf. Belsky and Gillovich, *Why Smart People Make Big Money Mistakes—and How to Correct Them*, 44.

12. www.familylands.com/article2.html.

13. Schott, *Mind Over Money*, 3; italics in the original.

14. Ibid..

15. Dennis T. Jaffe and James A. Grubman, "Acquirers' and Inheritors' Dilemma: Discovering Life Purpose and Building Personal Identity in the Presence of Wealth." *Journal of Wealth Management* 10 (2007): 20–44.

16. Ibid., 21.

17. Ibid.

18. Cf. A. Greenspan, "Economic Development and Financial Literacy." Ninth Annual Economic Development Summit, The Greenlining Institute, Oakland, California, January 10, 2002. Also, A. Greenspan, *The Age of Turbulence* (New York: Penguin, 2007).

19. R. T. Kiyosaki and S. L. Lechter, *Rich Dad, Poor Dad: What the Rich Teach Their Kids about Money—That the Poor and Middle Class Do Not!* (New York: Warner Books, 2000).

## Chapter 3: Know Yourself

1. N. Kagan, "Influencing Human Interaction—Eighteen Years with IPR." In A. K. Hess (ed.), *Psychotherapy Supervision: Theory, Research, and Practice* (New York: Wiley, 1980): 262–283.

2. Craig S. Cashwell, "IPR: Revealing Thoughts and Feelings in Supervision." www.cyc-net.org/cyc-online/cycol-1001-supervision.html.

## Chapter 4: Service Model Supporting Life Outcomes

1. CapGemini/Merrill Lynch, *World Wealth Report*, 2007: 26.

2. Ibid., 27.

3. I draw heavily from the work of The Legacy Companies, LLC, here and Scott Fithian's, *Values-Based Estate Planning*. The four processes described below are from G. Scott Budge, "Continuing Challenges to Delivering Wealth Management Services to Business Owners," *Journal of Wealth Management* 10 (2007): 51–62.
4. Cf. M. Anantharaman, "Millionaires Turn to Psychologists. *Yahoo News*, October 9, 2007. http://news.yahoo.com/s/nm/20071009/bs_nm/wealth_summit_psychol.
5. Jay R. Galbraith, "Organizing to Deliver Solutions," *Organizational Dynamics* 31(2) (2002): 194–207.
6. Interview with Keith Whitaker, Wachovia (Calibre), September 9, 2007.

## Chapter 5: Facilitating Family Meetings

1. Craig E. Aronoff, "Megatrends in Family Business," *Family Business Review* 11 (1998): 181–186.
2. Many have found the various works of Edward Tufte to be very instructive on how to visually organize mathematical and statistical information. See, for example, *The Visual Display of Quantitative Information* (Cheshire, CT: Graphics Press, 1999) and *Envisioning Information* (Cheshire, CT: Graphics Press, 1990) as representations of his approach to presenting complex information to various types of consumers.

## Chapter 6: Major Life Events: How You Can Help Families Navigate Difficult Times

1. The death of a child-The grief of the parents: A lifetime journey. http://www.athealth.com/consumer/disorders/parentalgrief.html
2. Ibid.
3. Interview with Peter White, former Vice Chairman of Bank of America US Trust. November 12, 2007.
4. Interview with Evan Roth, Partner, BBR Partners, LLC, November 12, 2007.
5. Excellent resources for the Sandwich Generation® can be found at Carol Abaya's website at htptp://www.thesandwichgeneration.com/.

## Chapter 8: Skill Development for Your New Role

1. James E. Hughes Jr., *Family: The Compact among Generations— Answers and Insights from a Lifetime of Helping Families Flourish* (New York: Bloomberg Press, 2007).
2. Ibid., 236–237.

3. Ibid., 237.

4. Stephanie Braverman, "Two, Four, Six, Eight, Let's All Differentiate Differential Education: Yesterday, Today, and Tomorrow," www.newhorizons.org/strategies/differentiated/bravmann.htm. Stephanie Braverman outlines the principles of differential education as follows: "Differentiation itself is based on three beliefs: 1. Everyone learns differently; 2. Quality is more important than quantity (e.g., significance trumps coverage); 3. "One-size-fits-all" curriculum and instruction presumes that content is more important than students. These beliefs, in turn, require that every teacher answer three specific questions: 1. In the content you must teach, what is it that you want all of your students to know?; 2. How can each student best learn this in ways that are appropriate to his/her specific needs?; 3. How can each student most effectively demonstrate what s/he has learned?"

5. Jay Hughes makes a point of using several devices with families, like the Structure of Intellect and 4MAT tools, to assist in the identification of learning styles in family members. The Legacy Companies' process, as another example, uses the Kolbe A to help assess approaches to decision-making and management.

6. Interview with Keith Whitaker, Wachovia (Calibre), September 9, 2007.

7. An interdisciplinary group of us founded this project in 1999 as a safe haven to explore with families their needs and issues around money in a context free of a product-sales agenda. More information about this project can be found at http://ackerman.org/centers/centerFor WorkAndFamily/moneyValuesAndFamilyLife.html

8. Edwin A. Hoover and Colette Lombard Hoover, *Getting Along in the Family Business: A Relationship Intelligence Handbook* (London: Routledge, 1999). See the chapter on RQ and Working with Family Businesses.

9. See, for example, C. E. Aronoff, J. L. Ward, and F. M. de Visscher, *Financing Transitions: Managing Capital and Liquidity in the Family Business* (Kennessaw, GA: Business Owner Resources, 1995) for a nice example of strategies that can work well in situations where tensions between control, capital, and liquidity can threaten the viability of the family business.

# Chapter 9: Ethical Considerations for Trusted Advisors

1. Taken from the FPA's Code of Ethics at www.fpanet.org/member/about/principles/Ethics.cfm.

2. See www.scu.edu/ethics/practicing/decision/framework.html, published by the Markkula Center for Applied Ethics.

# Index